Tube Trails

In association with London Transport

By the same authors

London for Free
London Fun Book
Edinburgh for Free
My Visit to Edinburgh
Dublin for Free

MARY PEPLOW
AND DEBRA SHIPLEY

Tube Trails

In association with London Transport

Illustrated by
Caroline Reeves

DRAGON

Dragon
An imprint of the Children's Division
of the Collins Publishing Group
8 Grafton Street, London W1X 3LA

Published by Dragon Books 1987

Text copyright © Mary Peplow and Debra Shipley 1987
Illustrations copyright © Caroline Reeves 1987

British Library Cataloguing in Publication Data
Peplow, Mary
    Tube trails.
    1. Subways – England – London – Stations
    – Juvenile literature
    I. Title   II. Shipley, Debra
    388.4'71'09421   HE4719.L7
    ISBN 0-583-31042-7

Printed and bound in Great Britain by
Cox & Wyman Ltd, Reading

Set in Plantin

CONTENTS

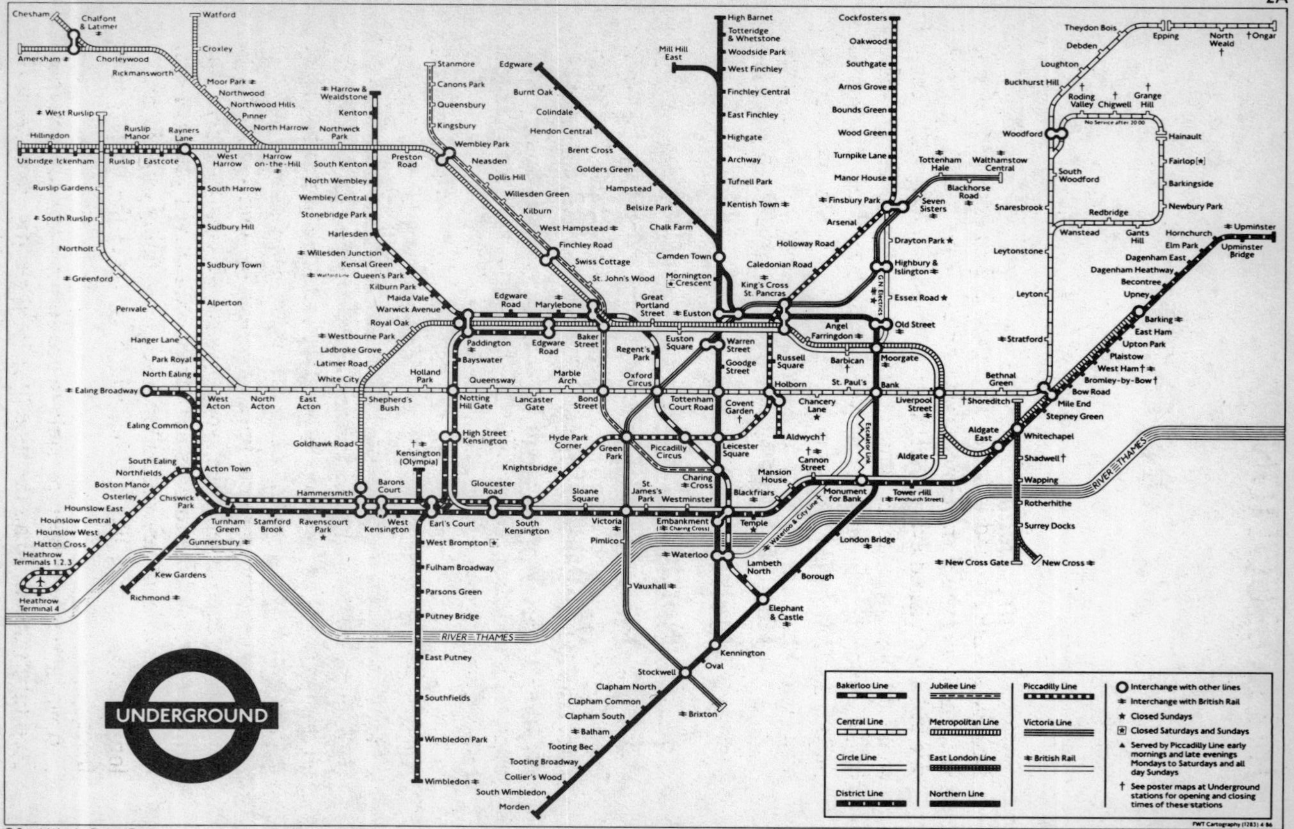

London Regional Transport Underground Map
Registered User No. 87/658

INTRODUCTION

London's Underground is huge! There are 272 stations and, if you visit them all, you'll travel about 244 miles. Want to give it a go? We did – we visited every one! All the stations are very different – some are big, some small, some are right out in the country, some in the centre of London – but we've written about them all. And to make your tube trails more fun we've tried to find somewhere to visit and something to spot at each station. But there are some stations where we didn't find anything. Can you help? If you can, please write and tell us about it.

There is one thing we should explain before you start your travels. People often call the Underground the Tube, but this word should only really be used for the six deep level lines. The other three, the Metropolitan, District and Circle Lines, are older and are not tubes at all. They were built by digging a trench, lining it with brick walls and then roofing over the tracks at ground level. This is called 'cut and cover' construction.

You will notice that none of the stations on the three cut and cover lines are very deep and you do not need to use lifts or escalators to reach the platforms. There are many open sections on these lines, even in central London. This is because the trains were all originally pulled by steam locomotives, so there had to be plenty of gaps in the tunnels to let out all the smoke and steam!

All the other Underground lines were built by tunnelling through the earth at deep level. Men working inside a circular shield dug out the earth, and the tunnels were lined with curved pieces of iron or concrete. When they were all in place these lining rings formed a long circular tunnel like a tube, which is where the name comes from.

It would not have been possible to use steam locomotives in these deep tube tunnels, so all the tube lines used electric trains from the start. The Northern, Central, Bakerloo, Piccadilly, Victoria and Jubilee Lines are all tubes, and have much smaller trains than the three cut and cover lines. Tube tunnels are only about 12 feet 6 inches (3.85 metres) in diameter, so there is not enough space for normal size trains. Just to confuse you a bit more, the larger trains used on the Metropolitan, District and Circle Lines are called 'surface stock', although of course they run underground as well as on the surface! The smaller trains are called 'tube stock'.

Less than half the Underground system is actually under the ground. There are 105 miles (167 kilometres) of route in tunnel, of which 20 miles are cut and cover, and 85 miles are in tube. The rest is overground – all 139 miles (223 kilometres) of it!

Got that? Happy tube (and cut and cover) trails!

BAKERLOO LINE

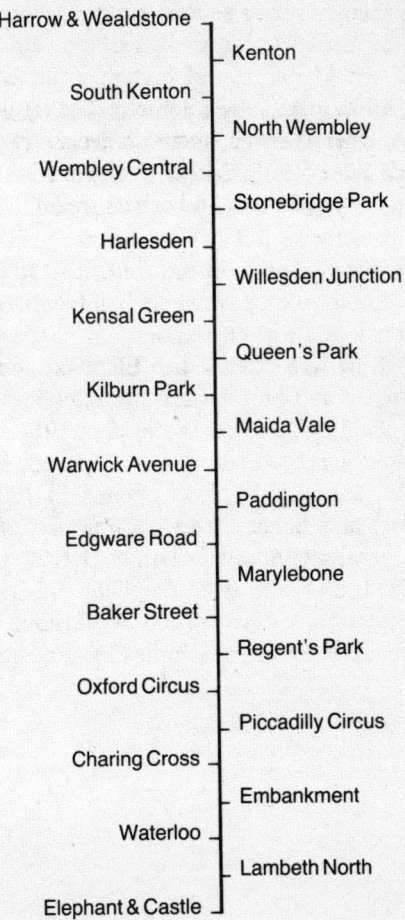

Harrow & Wealdstone

Kenton

South Kenton

North Wembley

Wembley Central

Stonebridge Park

Harlesden

Willesden Junction

Kensal Green

Queen's Park

Kilburn Park

Maida Vale

Warwick Avenue

Paddington

Edgware Road

Marylebone

Baker Street

Regent's Park

Oxford Circus

Piccadilly Circus

Charing Cross

Embankment

Waterloo

Lambeth North

Elephant & Castle

The **Bakerloo Line** was built by a company called the Baker Street and Waterloo Railway. The first section – between Baker Street and Kennington Road (now Lambeth North) was opened on 10th March 1906. To begin with, it wasn't very successful with only about 20,000–30,000 passengers a day. However, business picked up when a new way of paying was introduced. Instead of the standard 2d (old pence) for a ride, passengers paid between 1d and 3d depending on how long their journey was.

The Bakerloo Line was extended to Elephant and Castle on 5th August 1906, to Great Central (now Marylebone) and Edgware Road on 15th June 1907, and to Watford in 1917. In 1939 a new branch from Baker Street to Stanmore was opened. However, when the Jubilee Line (see page 76) was opened in 1979, the section between Stanmore and Baker Street became part of the new line. The Bakerloo Line was withdrawn north of Harrow and Wealdstone on 4th June 1984. It now runs from Elephant and Castle to Queen's Park, with an extension to Harrow and Wealdstone in peak hours. That means that it covers 14 route miles in peak hours and serves 25 stations.

Elephant and Castle

To know Elephant and Castle gets its name from an old tavern which once stood here. On the front of the tavern there was a gilt model of an elephant and a castle – the tavern quickly became known as the Elephant and Castle. The station was opened for the Northern Line on 18th December 1890, and for the Bakerloo Line on 5th August 1906.

To see Inside the Imperial War Museum (Lambeth Road, SE1 Tel: 01-735 8922) there are all sorts of weapons, medals and even tanks. Outside two fifteen inch naval guns point out over the Lambeth Road.

Nearby is the Elephant and Castle Recreation Centre (22 Elephant and Castle, SE1 Tel: 01-582 5505). By the swimming pool there's a pink elephant!

To spot The popular gilt models, saved when the Elephant and Castle Tavern was demolished in 1959, in front of the shopping centre.

Lambeth North

To know The name Lambeth comes from two old English words, 'lam' meaning dirt or mud, and 'hythe' meaning a haven. The

11

underground station was opened here on 10th March 1906 and was originally called Kennington Road. It was renamed Westminster Bridge Road on 5th August 1906 and finally named Lambeth North on 15th April 1917.

To see You can visit the only Museum of Garden History in the world at St Mary-at-Lambeth (Lambeth Palace Road, SE1 Tel: 01-261 1891). In its churchyard/garden you can see the tomb of William Bligh (1754–1817) who was Captain of the 'Bounty'.

To spot Lambeth Palace, next to the Museum of Garden History. It is the London home of the Archbishop of Canterbury. (Not open to the public.)

Waterloo

To know A staggering 28 million people each year either begin or end their journeys on the underground at Waterloo, which was opened for the Bakerloo Line on 10th March 1906; the Northern Line platforms were opened on 13th September 1926. As you leave the station travelling south on the Northern Line you'll be some 70 feet (21.3 metres) below sea level.

To see Waterloo Bridge has perhaps the best views of London, eastwards down the Thames to the City and west towards the Houses of Parliament. From the bridge take the steps down to the riverside walkway – the South Bank. From here you can visit the Royal Festival Hall and the National Theatre – both have free exhibitions in their foyers – and the National Film Theatre. A new museum of film and television is opening here in 1988, the Museum of the Moving Image. But there's lots to see outside as you walk beside the water. Look out for ditties written on the paving stones and for stone elephants in Jubilee Gardens.

To spot A brightly coloured sculpture on the top of the Hayward Gallery.

Embankment

To know The station was originally Embankment and Charing Cross (see below) but became just Embankment on 10th March 1906.

To see Victoria Embankment Gardens (SW1, WC2), just a few minutes' walk away. There are fountains, a lily pond and a bandstand. This area was part of the River Thames until the 1860s when the Embankment was built. The York Water Gate in the gardens marks the original shore line of the river. Can you find it?

To spot Statues in Victoria Embankment Gardens. How many are there and who are they of?

Charing Cross

To know Running the full length of the Bakerloo Line platform, about 350 feet (107 metres), there are spectacular murals based on paintings from the National Gallery and the National Portrait Gallery nearby. On the Northern Line platforms too, there are murals – telling the story of the original Eleanor Cross from which the underground station takes its name. The first Eleanor Cross, which was made from wood, was erected almost 700 years ago by King Edward I in memory of his wife, Queen Eleanor of Castile. The present cross (which you can see outside Charing Cross British Rail station) was made during the 19th Century. The station was originally opened as Trafalgar Square on 10th March 1906. It was renamed Charing Cross in 1979.

To see The National Gallery (Trafalgar Square, WC2 Tel: 01-839 3321). It has a very large collection of paintings which date back to 1300. You can usually pick up a quiz sheet in the gallery foyer and test your knowledge! Look out for a painting of a tiger in the rain ('Tropical Storm with a Tiger' by Rousseau), because you can also see it reproduced as a wall decoration at Charing Cross underground.

To spot Trafalgar Square (WC2), with its 185 feet (56.4 metres) high Nelson's Column. How many lions are there at its base?

Piccadilly Circus

To know The station was opened on 10th March 1906. It was rebuilt and reopened on 10th December 1928, and is now being modernized again.

To visit Piccadilly Circus, one of the busiest parts of London. From here you can visit the Trocadero – a lively shopping complex which has lots of cafés. It houses the Guinness World of Records, a display of world-record breaking events and breathtaking achievements. You'll be astounded by some of the feats carried out and astonished by some of the records established. How about the gentleman who, in 1979, dived 28 feet (8.6 metres) into just 12¾ inches (32 centimetres) of water! Or the heaviest man in the world – he tops the scales at a massive 76 stones (483 kg)! Perhaps you'll be inspired to try and break a record yourself.

To spot You can't miss Eros! The subject of thousands and thousands of post-cards and almost as well known as the red double decker bus or the black taxi cab, this small, but famous statue is very much a part of the razzmatazz of Piccadilly Circus.

Oxford Circus

To know The Central Line station was opened on 30th July 1900 and the Bakerloo on 10 March 1906. Oxford Circus has more escalators than any underground station in London – there are 14!

To see Oxford Street, one of the best known shopping streets in London. It's especially pretty around Christmas time when there are bright decorations everywhere. Hamleys, the largest toyshop in the world, is close by in Regent Street. Tucked away from all the busy shops is the Museum of Mankind (6, Burlington Gardens, W1 Tel: 01-437 2224/8) where you can find out all about the lifestyle and culture of different peoples from all over the world. Look out for the gold badge worn by attendants of the Ashanti kings.

To spot Liberty's, as pretty from the outside as it is from the inside. You can't miss it, it's the black and white building at the end of Argyll Street.

Regent's Park

To know The station was opened on 10th March 1906.

To see London Zoo (Regent's Park, NW1 Tel: 01-722 3333). Walk through Regent's Park and you'll see all the signs pointing the way. There are over 9,000 different animals here – lions, elephants, monkeys and apes. You can see them very close-up but don't feed them – the animals are all on special diets to keep them healthy. If you're lucky you might be there at feeding time – it's quite a sight!

To spot Regent's Park, opposite the station – but do use the subway to cross the busy road.

Baker Street

To know There are ten platforms here. Only one other station on the underground has so many – and that's Moorgate (page 53). Five lines run through the station. The first was the Metropolitan Line which was opened on 10th January 1863. The 'extension' line was added five years later. The Bakerloo Line was built in 1906 and the Jubilee line in 1979.

To see Just a few minutes walk away is the London Planetarium (Tel: 01-486 1121) where you can look up into the starry night skies, and find out more about famous astronomers. Next to the Planetarium is Madame Tussauds (Tel: 01-935 6861) with its gruesome Chamber of Horrors and exhibitions of lifesize wax figures of well-known personalities – past and present – sportspeople, royalty, pop stars and politicians . . .

To spot Sherlock Holmes, the world's best-known fictional detective. His address was 221b Baker Street. You'll find drawings of him and other characters in the stories on the Jubilee Line platform and silhouettes of his head – with deer stalker and pipe, of course – on wall tiles around the inside of the station.

Marylebone

To know The station was first called Great Central when it was opened on 27th March 1907. It was renamed Marylebone on 15th April 1917.

To spot The big archway at the entrance. Marylebone is also a main line station. Look for the initials of the company that built it – the Great Central Railway – on the railings outside.

Edgware Road

To know The station was opened on 15th June 1907

To see You'll find an amazing selection of all sorts of bits and bobs on sale at nearby Church Street Market, open Tuesday to Saturday, but best on Saturday mornings. It's fun hearing all the street cries!

To spot The huge police station opposite.

Paddington

To know There are two underground stations at Paddington connected by the main line railway station. The first, which has Metropolitan, Circle and District Lines running through, was opened on 1st October 1868. The Bakerloo Line station was opened on 1st December 1913.

To see Paddington Station itself is fascinating. It covers 13 acres, and it's estimated that some 48,000 passengers, 27,000 parcels and 10,000 mail bags pass through it each day – so there's always something going on! Apparently, Queen Victoria travelled from Slough to Paddington Station on her first railway journey. It was 17 miles and took 23 minutes – and Prince Albert thought it was far too speedy. 'Not so fast next time, Mr Conductor,' he said when they arrived!

To spot A statue of Brunel, the famous railway engineer, just outside the entrance to the tube in the main-line station. And look out for the huge statue of a soldier on Platform 1.

Warwick Avenue

To know The station was opened on 31st January 1915

To see 'Jason' – a colourfully painted narrowboat, just a few minutes walk away. It is ready to take you along Regent's Canal around Brownings Island, down Maida Hill Tunnel, under Blow Up Bridge, through the Zoo, past Pirates Castle to Camden Lock and then back to Little Venice. For the departure times (summer months only), you should contact Jason's Trip, Little Venice, London W9 (Tel: 01-286 3428).

Maida Vale

To know The station was opened on 6th June 1915 during World War I. Because so many men were fighting abroad, the station was staffed entirely by women.

To spot The old underground sign in mosaic. As you go into the station entrance look to your right.

Kilburn Park

To know The station was opened on 31st January 1915.

To spot Royalty nearby – at least a picture of a prince, The Prince of Wales!

Queen's Park

To know The first station to stand on this site was called Queen's Park (West Kilburn). It was opened on 2nd June 1879 for mainline trains of the London and North Western Railway. A new station was built and opened on 11th February 1915.

To see Queen's Park itself is a 30 acre park with tennis courts, a pitch and putt course and a playground. There is a lovely bandstand in the centre.

To spot A set of weighing scales on the platform. How much do you weigh?

Kensal Green

To know The station was opened on 1st October 1916. It was reconstructed and reopened on 3rd February 1981.

To spot Kensal Green Cemetery nearby, where many famous Victorians are buried, including Brunel.

Willesden Junction

To know There is a railway junction here which is why the station is called Willesden Junction. It was opened by the London and North Western Railway on 1st September 1866 but not used by underground trains until 10th May 1915.

To spot An Edward VII letter box opposite the booking office.

Harlesden

To know The station was first used by underground trains on 16th April 1917.

To spot Huge cooling towers nearby. How many can you spot?

Stonebridge Park

To know The station was opened by the London and North Western Railway on 15th June 1912 and first used by underground trains on 16th April 1917.

To spot Walk up onto the stone bridge on the station and you'll see all the main-line trains coming and going.

Wembley Central

To know The station was first used for underground trains on 16th April 1917. At that time it was known as Wembley for Sudbury. It was renamed Wembley Central on 5th July 1948.

To spot A bright orange slide which looks like something from outer space in the centre of the station's shopping area.

North Wembley

To know Although the station was opened on 15th June 1912 by the London and North Western Railway, it wasn't used by underground trains until 16th April 1917.

To spot Look to your left – can you see a dog chasing a duck?

South Kenton

To know The station was opened on 3rd July 1933.

To spot A beautiful view of Harrow-on-the-Hill with a little church on top. The hill is about 300 feet (92 metres) high.

Kenton

To know The station was first used by underground trains on 16th April 1917.

To spot 'Puffers', just over the bridge. You'll get a treat if you look inside this shop window!

Harrow and Wealdstone

To know The station was first used by underground trains on 16th April 1917 although it had been open since 20th July 1837 for main-line trains of the London and Birmingham Railway.

To see The Harrow Leisure Centre nearby in Christchurch Avenue, (Tel: 01-863 5611). If you want to play badminton, table tennis or go for a swim, you're in luck. There's also a roller-skating arena – so get your skates on!

To spot A luggage trolley from the station's main-line days, put to a very colourful use – as a flower bed!

CENTRAL LINE

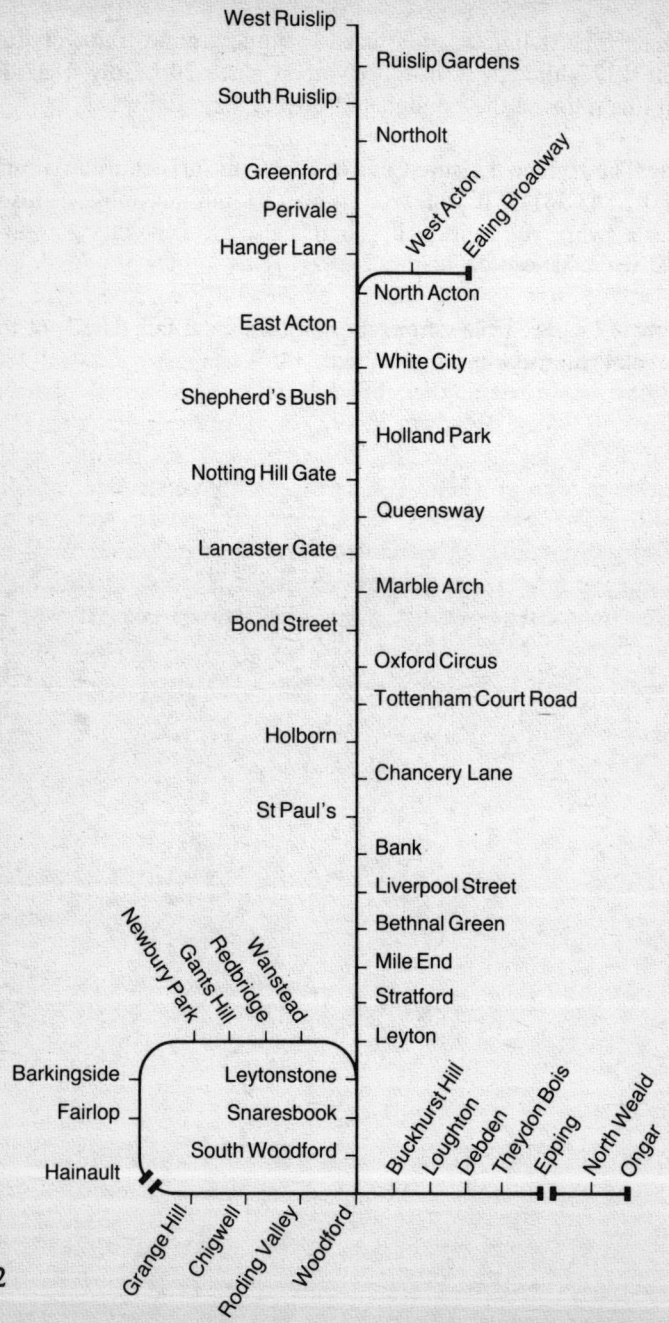

West Ruislip
Ruislip Gardens
South Ruislip
Northolt
Greenford
Perivale
Hanger Lane
West Acton
Ealing Broadway
North Acton
East Acton
White City
Shepherd's Bush
Holland Park
Notting Hill Gate
Queensway
Lancaster Gate
Marble Arch
Bond Street
Oxford Circus
Tottenham Court Road
Holborn
Chancery Lane
St Paul's
Bank
Liverpool Street
Bethnal Green
Mile End
Stratford
Leyton
Newbury Park
Gants Hill
Redbridge
Wanstead
Barkingside
Leytonstone
Fairlop
Snaresbook
South Woodford
Hainault
Buckhurst Hill
Loughton
Debden
Theydon Bois
Epping
North Weald
Ongar
Grange Hill
Chigwell
Roding Valley
Woodford

When the first section of the **Central Line** – between Bank and Shepherd's Bush – was opened in 1900 it was known as the 'Tuppenny Tube' because passengers paid a flat fare of 2d. It was given a royal opening by the Prince of Wales (later Edward VII) and trains began running on 30th July 1900. The Central Line was extended to Ealing Broadway in 1920 and plans were later made to extend it to Ongar and Ruislip. However, work was stopped by the outbreak of war in 1939. The newly-built tunnels were quickly adapted as air raid shelters, bomb-proof stores and factories for making war materials. After the war, extensions continued and the Central Line now covers 52 route miles and stops at 51 stations. It runs between Ealing Broadway or West Ruislip and Hainault or Epping, with a shuttle service from Woodford to Hainault, and a peak hour shuttle service from Epping to Ongar.

West Ruislip

To know The longest journey without changing tubes is between Epping (see page 40) and West Ruislip. From end to end it's 34.1 miles.

To spot A train-wash system a little to the east of the platform. You can get a good look at it from inside the tube as it approaches the station.

Ruislip Gardens

To know The station was opened here on 21st November 1948.

To spot The river which passes beneath the tube lines.

South Ruislip

To know On the 21st November 1948 the underground station was opened.

To spot British Rail trains rush through South Ruislip, running beside the underground line – so you can do some train spotting from here.

Northolt

To know Northolt station was opened on 21st November 1948.

Greenford

To know A station was opened here on 1st October 1904 by the Great Western Railway. Underground trains first used it on 30th June 1947.

To see Part of the Grand Union canal passes near Greenford. It was the M1 of its day, linking the industrial Midlands with London. You could easily spend a whole day exploring the canal towpaths (it's best to go with a group of friends and don't be tempted to take a dip – the water is both polluted and dangerous, filled with lots of scrap metal and old cans). There's plenty to see including lots of wildlife.

To spot A gasometer from the platform. Is it to the north, south, east or west of the station?

Perivale

To know The station was opened for underground trains on 30th June 1947.

To see Perivale Park is near the tube station. Which river runs through it?

To spot CBS/Fox Videos have large modern premises near the tube line. Can you spot which other company is nearby?

Hanger Lane

To know The underground was opened here on 30th June 1947.

To see Perhaps you've heard the DJ on one of London's local radio stations mention the Hanger Lane gyratory system? It's well known with motorists who've had to sit in traffic jams caused by it. Can you find out what it is?

To spot A large building near the station with the letters AGB. Can you discover what they stand for?

Ealing Broadway

To know District Line underground trains first used this station on 1st July 1879, and Central Line tube trains on 3rd August 1920.

To see There are often buskers, mime shows and clowns at the weekend in Ealing Shopping Centre – it makes shopping much more fun!

To spot A huge black and white building to the right of the station entrance. It's called Villiers House. This is where BBC producers, directors and researchers work on some of your favourite television programmes.

West Acton

To know The station was opened on 5th November 1923.

North Acton

To know The underground station was opened here on 5th November 1923.

To spot Landris and Gyr, an engineering firm, have a factory alongside the station. What's unusual about the wall you can see from the platform?

East Acton

To know The underground station was opened here on 3rd August 1920.

To spot From the platform you can see a modern church spire – it's topped by a cross. See if you can find the road which leads to it and discover its name.

White City

To know The original Central Line station near here was called Wood Lane, opened on 14th May 1908. This was closed when the present station at White City was opened on 23rd November 1947.

The name White City comes from a huge exhibition held here in 1908 where all the buildings were white.

To see There's a fantastic leisure pool nearby called The White City Pool (Bloemfontein Road, W12 Tel: 01-743 3401). It's got a wave machine, a diving pit and bumper boats. Have a splashing time!

To spot The old Wood Lane station. You can see the platform from a westbound train just before you arrive at White City. Turn left outside White City and you will find the old station entrance. What is the big building opposite? (Here's a clue: it's the home of Blue Peter.)

Shepherd's Bush

To know The station was opened on 30th July 1900.

To spot The sheep coming down a country lane. They're on the wall opposite the escalators!

Holland Park

To know The station was opened on 30th July 1900.

To see You'll find lots of rabbits hopping about in Holland Park – there are squirrels and ducks, and beautiful peacocks too. You can have great fun exploring the woodland and spotting all the different trees and birds. If it's raining you can shelter in the old Orangery which often has art displays. Nearby is Leighton House (12 Holland Park Road, W14 Tel: 01-602 3316) which is a small museum with lots of very special Victorian paintings. Look out for the sunken fountain!

To spot Some very pretty wrought ironwork at the station. Look up as you walk off the platform to the stairs.

Notting Hill Gate

To know The District Line station was opened on 1st October 1868 and the Central Line on 30th July 1900. The two were linked together in 1959.

To see Notting Hill Gate Carnival is one of the biggest, brightest and noisiest carnivals in London. The streets in the Notting Hill area are full of people dancing and singing. Everyone dresses up for the occasion in amazing costumes and there are bands, floats, side-shows and lots, lots more. It's held on the three days over August Bank Holiday and it's great fun to join in – but do stay close to your family or friends, it's very easy to get lost.

Portobello Road nearby has a street market and lots of antique shops.

To spot A picture of a Coat of Arms on a wall near the station. Which family does it belong to? And in Portobello Road, one of the oldest cinemas in London, opened in 1905. What is it called?

Queensway

To know It was opened as Queen's Road on 30th July 1900, then renamed Queensway on 1st September 1946. The road, Queensway, was named in honour of Queen Victoria. Apparently she used to ride along it on a horse when she was a child!

To see Enjoy yourself in Kensington Gardens – just opposite the station! Don't miss the Pets' Cemetery where much-loved pets have been buried since 1880. And the statue of Peter Pan blowing his horn. What can you see clustered around the bottom of the statue? Look out for model boats on the Round Pond.

To spot As you come into the station there's a crown painted on the tiles in red and white. There's another somewhere in the station – can you find it?

Lancaster Gate

To know It was opened on 30th July 1900.

To see You'll find an amazing collection of model trains from all over the world – including old trains from the Paris Metro and the Berlin Underground – at The London Toy and Model Museum (23

Craven Hill, W2 Tel: 01-262 7905/9450). But it's not only trains –
there are lots of penny toys, dolls, teddy bears, music sheets, a
beautiful doll's house and the shop fronts of famous toy companies.

To spot Flags flying from the top of the Royal Lancaster Hotel. Do
you know which countries they represent?

Marble Arch

To know The station was opened on 30th July 1900. It gets its name
from Marble Arch which is just opposite the station. This huge
arch was built as a gateway to Buckingham Palace but everyone
said that it was too narrow so it became an entrance to Hyde Park
instead. But as you can see, it doesn't serve much purpose now –
except as a famous landmark!

To see Have you got anything important to say? Well, there's an
area near the station known as 'Speakers' Corner' where you can
stand up and say whatever you like! People stand on orange boxes
and talk about religion, politics, poetry . . . it's great fun to listen.
Hyde Park itself is enormous – about 361 acres in all. One of the
best places in the park is the Serpentine, a lake where you can swim
(at the Lido), row, sail and fish. The ducks here are always hungry
– so take some stale bread to feed them.

To spot There's a brass plaque near the station which marks the site where the Tyburn Tree used to stand. These were gallows used for hanging heretics, highwaymen and thieves. They were so big that 24 people could be hanged at the same time.

Bond Street

To know The Central Line station was opened on 24th September 1900.

To see This is one of the most fashionable shopping areas in London with shops selling expensive things such as furs, Persian rugs and rare prints. Look out for Sotheby's, the famous auctioneers, at 34–35 New Bond Street. Even if you're not interested in shopping you should try to visit Burlington Arcade with its tiny little shops and very tall Beadles. But be careful – there's a law forbidding singing and running or carrying open umbrellas or parcels, and the Beadles are there to make sure you don't forget it! They are actually the smallest police force in the world! Not far away is Grosvenor Square where you can see the huge building of the United States Embassy with the golden eagle on top.

To spot Just in case you'd forgotten where you are – the name of the station is repeated over and over on the tiles of the Central Line platform!

Oxford Circus (see Bakerloo Line page 15)

Tottenham Court Road

To know The Central Line was opened here on 30th July 1900 and the Northern Line (known first as Oxford Street but renamed Tottenham Court Road) on 22nd June 1907.

To see The British Museum (Great Russell Street, WC1 Tel: 01-636 1555) is packed full of fascinating things. You may have learnt about some of them in school – the Sutton Hoo Burial Ship; the Rosetta Stone. There are also lots of Egyptian mummies, oriental china and illuminated books (books decorated with intricate, hand-painted designs).

To spot The mosaic design, by artist Eduardo Paolozzi. It is a blaze of colour and makes Tottenham Court Road surely the most colourful of all the underground stations. Can you find the butterfly?

Holborn

To know The Piccadilly Line station was opened on 15th December 1906. The Central Line platforms were opened on 25th September 1933.

To see Lincoln's Inn Fields, near Holborn tube station, is now a good place to eat your sandwiches, but once this was where people were executed. At number 13 is the Sir John Soane's Museum (Tel: 01-405 2107). An amazing place to visit, it is full of mirrors and walls which are not walls. You'll soon get lost in what is really quite a small house. Look out for the Egyptian sarcophagus. It's so big that a wall had to be taken down to get it inside the museum!

To spot Take a close look at the offices of the Nationwide Building Society in High Holborn. At night its lights change colour! Now take a close look at the building next to it on the right, which now contains a sandwich bar. This was originally British Museum tube station, closed in 1933.

Chancery Lane

To know The escalator here is the shortest in the underground system, just 30 feet (9.1 metres). Its vertical rise is only 15 feet (4.6 metres) and its length, comb-to-comb, about 39 feet (11.9 metres). A station was first opened here on 30th July 1900 and the present 'new' one on 25th June 1934.

To see Highly polished silver of every kind is on show in the London Silver Vaults (Chancery Lane, WC2). Nearby, Leather Lane Market is a real contrast – every sort of bric-à-brac is sold here at 'knock down' prices.

To spot Griffins on guard outside the tube! Actually they mark the boundary of the City of London.

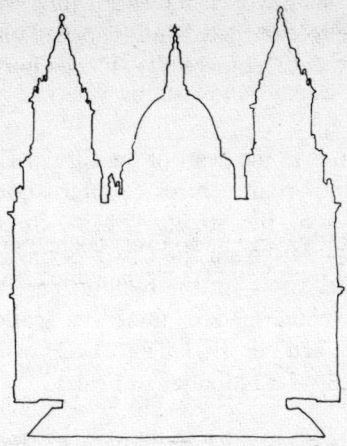

St Paul's

To know Opened on 30th July 1900, this station was originally called Post Office, but was renamed St Paul's on 1st February 1937.

To see Designed by Sir Christopher Wren after the Great Fire of London, St Paul's is the cathedral where the Prince of Wales and Lady Diana Spencer were married in 1981. Try standing in its gallery and whispering to a friend on the other side – 107 feet (32.6 metres) away . . .

To spot A colourful map of north Africa, with a horse and a camel – just outside the station.

Bank

To know The station takes its name from the Bank of England which was established in the City of London in 1694. There are lots of dates associated with Bank underground station:
– Waterloo and City Line opened 11th July 1898. This station, which was called City, was renamed Bank on 28th October 1940

- the Northern Line station was opened on 25th February 1900 (it was then called the City and South London Railway)
- the Central Line station opened on 30th July 1900
- the stations were reconstructed and reopened on 5th May 1925
- the Bank/Monument (see page 51) subway opened on 18th September 1933.

To see Bank station is in the heart of the City of London, one of the oldest and most important centres of international finance in the world. The names of the streets – Milk Street, Bread Street, Draper's Gardens – date from the City's beginnings as a centre of trade in the Middle Ages, but the buildings are the latest in high-tech. You can see some modern traders at work if you visit The Royal Exchange (Cornhill, EC3 Tel: 01-623 0444). The Visitors' Gallery is open 11.30–1.30 Monday to Friday.

To spot Can you discover which building is the Bank of England? It has a rather nice nickname which will give you a clue, 'The Old Lady of Threadneedle Street'.

Liverpool Street

To know This was, in 1246, the site of a priory. Later it became the Bethlehem Hospital which stood until 1676. The Metropolitan Line underground station was opened on 12th July 1875 and was called Bishopsgate, but it was renamed Liverpool Street on 1st November 1909. The Central Line station was opened on 28th July 1912.

To see In the Geffrye Museum (Kingsland Road, E2 Tel: 01-739 8368), a short bus ride away, you can discover how a typical family would have lived and furnished their home from 1600–1939.

Bethnal Green

To know The station was opened on 4th December 1946.

To see Don't miss The Bethnal Green Museum of Childhood (Cambridge Heath Road, E2 Tel: 01-980 2415). There are fascinating old model theatres, peep-shows, puppets, dolls and rocking horses, to name but a few of its marvels. Look out for the doll's house which dates right back to 1673, and the Punch and Judy booth used from 1912 to 1962.

Mile End

To know Can you guess how Mile End got its name? It may be hard to imagine now, but way back in 1288 this was the main route from London to Colchester. Mile End marks the place roughly one mile from Aldgate. The District Line station was opened here on 2nd June 1902. It was rebuilt to take Central Line trains from 4th December 1946.

To spot The Royal Green Jackets' Territorial Army Headquarters opposite the entrance to the underground.

Stratford

To know On 20th June 1839 the Eastern Counties Railway opened a railway station here. The present underground station was opened on 4th December 1946.

To see Passmore Edwards Museum (Romford Road, E15 Tel: 01-519 4296), the local history museum for Newham, is a fascinating place to visit – particularly if you come from this part of London.

To spot The red-bricked Stratford Centre, just glimpsed amidst the criss-cross of railway lines and the jungle of industrial buildings around the station.

Leyton

To know Eastern Counties Railway opened a station here, called Low Leyton, on 22nd August 1856. It was renamed Leyton on 1st January 1864 and was first used by underground trains on 5th May 1947.

To see Eastway Sports Centre (Quartermile Lane, Leyton, E11 Tel: 01-519 0017) has an exciting range of activities including badminton, table tennis, volleyball and gymnastics.

To spot A cemetery with row after row of white-grey grave stones, if you look out of the window of the tube.

Leytonstone

To know The station was opened by Eastern Counties Railway on 22nd August 1856. It was first used by underground trains on 5th May 1947.

To spot A church spire above 'Bee's Tea Parlour' – what's the name of the church?

Wanstead

To know The station was opened on 14th December 1946.

Redbridge

To know Redbridge gets its name from an old red bridge which once crossed the river Roding here – it's marked on a map dated 1746. The station was opened on the 14th December 1947.

Gants Hill

To know During World War II London was bombed so much that people took to the underground's tunnels for safety. Between Gants

Hill and Leytonstone (see page 36) there are 5 miles of tunnels which had just been built when the war started. They were converted into an underground factory for the Plessey company to make aircraft components. After the war, tracks were laid, and the station was opened on 14th December 1947.

Newbury Park

To know Underground trains first used the station on 14th December 1947, but it was opened on 1st May 1903 by the Great Eastern Railway.

To spot The arched concrete bus station outside the tube station. This design won a special prize at the Festival of Britain in 1951. Can you find the plaque which tells you about it?

Barkingside

To know Barkingside, which was opened by the Great Eastern Railway on 1st May 1903, was first used by underground trains on 31st May 1948.

Fairlop

To know Fairlop is an unusual name for an underground station, but there's an interesting tale about where it comes from – can you guess? Try reading it as two separate words – 'fair' and 'lop'. Any ideas? Well, legend has it that there was once a fine Oak tree growing here. It was very large and sheltered a fairground owned by a man called Daniel Day. When Daniel died, his friends decided to make a coffin for him with wood from the oak. After they had cut the tree down, it started to grow again so they decided they must have made a fair (or good) lop (or cut). Local people put the two words together and soon called the area Fairlop!

The station was opened by the Great Eastern Railway on 1st May 1903 and was first used by underground trains on 31st May 1948.

Snaresbrook

To know Originally called Snaresbrook and Wanstead, the station was opened by the Eastern Counties Railway on 22nd August 1856. It was first used by underground trains and renamed Snaresbrook on 14th December 1947.

To see Epping Forest is really fantastic to explore with a group of friends, but you'll need a map to find your way through – it's massive! It was once a royal hunting forest and you can visit Queen Elizabeth I's hunting lodge and maybe even catch a glimpse of some deer. Particularly good places to eat your packed lunch are Baldwins Hill Pond and The Lost Pond. *Never* walk in Epping Forest on your own.

To spot Some cart-wheel shaped ironwork in the station. What's it part of?

South Woodford

To know This station was called George Lane when it was opened by the Eastern Counties Railway on 22nd August 1856. It was renamed South Woodford (George Lane) on 5th July 1937 and was first used by underground trains on 14th December 1947. It finally became simply South Woodford in 1950.

To spot The former station name plate on the platform wall – 'George Lane.'

Woodford

To know Years ago, when the whole area was covered with thick forest, this was the place where the river Roding could be crossed – hence its name 'wood' 'ford'. The station was opened by the Eastern Counties Railway on 22nd August 1856 and was first used by underground trains on 14th December 1947.

Buckhurst Hill

To know The station was first used by underground trains on 21st November 1948.

Loughton

To know The Eastern Counties Railway opened a station here on 22nd August 1856. A few years later in 1865, it was resited and later still in 1940 a new station was opened. It was first used by underground trains on 21st November 1948.

To spot A small coal dump near the station, from your vantage point inside the tube.

Debden

To know Opened by the Great Eastern Railway on 24th May 1865, this station was originally called Chigwell Road. It was renamed Chigwell Lane a few months later on 1st December 1867. Its name was changed yet again, this time to Debden, on 25th September 1949 – when it was first used by underground trains.

To spot Open hills in the surrounding area, reminding you that you're well on your way out of London. In fact you're in the county of Essex now.

Theydon Bois

To know The station was opened here, as Theydon, by the Great Eastern Railway on 24th April 1865. It was renamed Theydon Bois on 1st December 1965 and underground trains first stopped here on 25th September 1949.

To spot From the footbridge you can see the M25 – the tube lines disappear under it!

Epping

To know The station was opened on 24th April 1865 by the Great Eastern Railway. It was first used by underground trains on 25th September 1949.

North Weald

To know On 24th April 1865, the station was opened by the Great Eastern Railway. It was first used by underground trains on 18th November 1957.

Ongar

To know Ongar is about 24 miles (39 km) from central London. The station was opened by the Great Eastern Railway on 24th April 1865 and was first used by underground trains on 18th November 1957.

Roding Valley

To know The station was opened on 3rd February 1936 by the London and North Eastern Railway. It was first used by underground trains on 21st November 1948.

Chigwell

To know Chigwell, once a small village, was mentioned in the Domesday Book. Underground trains first used the station here on 21st November 1948.

Grange Hill

To know There was once a priory on the land here. A manor belonging to it was called 'The Grange'. The station opened by the Great Eastern Railway on 1st May 1903 and first used by underground trains on 21st November 1948, was named after it.

Hainault

To know The Great Eastern Railway opened a station at Hainault on 1st May 1903. It was first used by underground trains on 31st May 1948.

To see Hainault Forest, some 1,100 acres, is all that remains of what was once the Great Forest of Essex. It's easy to get lost here, so try following one of the two signposted walks and never go alone. With a fishing lake, boating, riding and a putting green, there's certainly plenty to do. Make sure you visit the paddocks where there are sheep, goats, pygmy donkeys and mountain ponies.

CIRCLE LINE

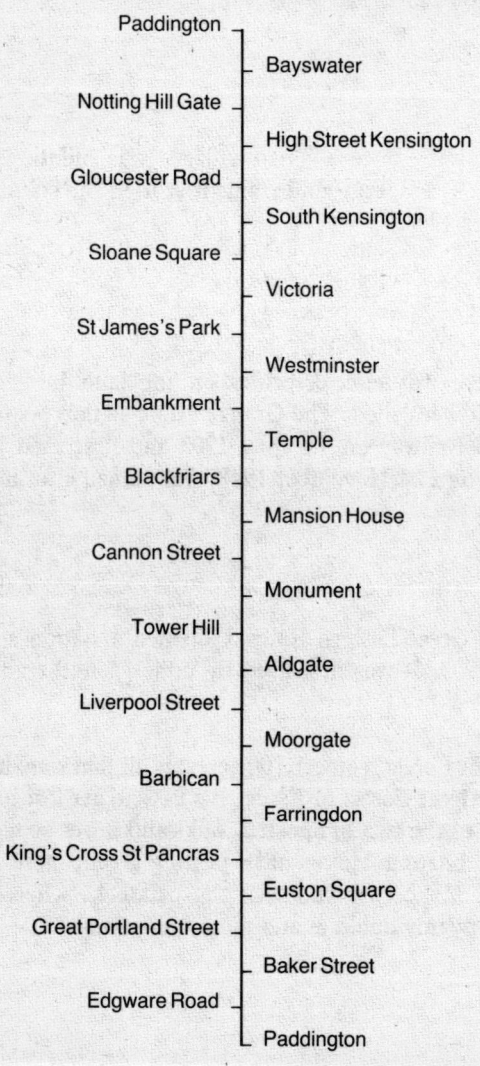

Paddington

Bayswater

Notting Hill Gate

High Street Kensington

Gloucester Road

South Kensington

Sloane Square

Victoria

St James's Park

Westminster

Embankment

Temple

Blackfriars

Mansion House

Cannon Street

Monument

Tower Hill

Aldgate

Liverpool Street

Moorgate

Barbican

Farringdon

King's Cross St Pancras

Euston Square

Great Portland Street

Baker Street

Edgware Road

Paddington

The **Circle Line** is a combination of the central sections of the Metropolitan and District Lines. If you look at an underground map you can see it more clearly. The Circle Line route is 13 miles long, stops at 27 stations and serves many of London's main-line stations such as Paddington and King's Cross/St Pancras.

The first section, between Paddington and Farringdon, was opened in 1863 by the Metropolitan Railway Company (see Metropolitan Line page 84). The section between South Kensington and Mansion House was built by another company, the Metropolitan District Railway (see District Line page 58). The final link to complete the circle was opened in 1884.

Until September 1905, steam trains were used on the Circle Line. When they introduced electric trains the journey was cut from 70 minutes to 50 minutes for a round trip. See how long it takes you today!

Paddington (see Bakerloo Line page 17)

Bayswater

To know When the station was first opened on 1st October 1868 it was called Bayswater. However, it later became known as Bayswater (Queen's Road), then as just Queen's Road, then Bayswater again, then back to Bayswater (Queen's Road), then Westbourne Grove, before coming back to Bayswater again in 1933!

Notting Hill Gate (see Central Line page 28)

High Street Kensington

To know The station was opened on 1st October 1868.

To see The Commonwealth Institute (Kensington High Street, W8 Tel: 01-603 3257). There are posters, charts, statues, costumes and films telling you all about the different countries in the Commonwealth and the lives of their people. And to test your knowledge, have a go at the special quiz. Nearby also is Kensington Palace (The Broad Walk, Kensington Gardens, W8 Tel: 01-212 3434) where you can take a peek at Queen Victoria's bedroom and see some of the costumes worn at Court since the 18th century. For more up to date clothes, go to Kensington Market in Kensington High Street, one of the most fashionable markets in London.

To spot As you walk past the ticket collector and into Kensington Arcade look up to the ceiling. There's a very modern 'chandelier' which looks like something out of a chemistry lesson!

Gloucester Road

To know The District Line station was opened as Brompton (Gloucester Road) on 1st October 1868, then renamed Gloucester

Road in 1907. The Piccadilly Line station was opened on 15th December 1906.

To see If you're a scout or girl-guide, you shouldn't miss Baden-Powell House (Queen's Gate, SW7 Tel: 01-584 7030) which has lots of exhibits and displays showing how the Scout Movement began and the work it has done over the years. There's a scale model of the car which was presented to Lord Baden-Powell at the Coming-of-Age Jamboree in 1929. He called it 'Jam Roll'!

To spot The station exit leads onto the busy, noisy Gloucester Road. As you watch the cars and lorries hurtling by, think back to the 18th century when this was a muddy road known as 'Hogmoore Lane'! The station still has its original 1868 buildings which have just been cleaned. Look out for the old District Railway lettering just below the roof on the outside.

South Kensington

To know The station was opened on 24th December 1868. The Piccadilly Line connection was opened on 8th January 1907.

To see You're in Museum Land! The problem is knowing where to go first so make sure you've left yourself plenty of time. You'll see the Crystal of Tourmaline and lots of other sparkling gems in The Geological Museum (Exhibition Road, SW7 Tel: 01-589 3444). The Natural History Museum (Cromwell Road, SW7 Tel: 01-589 6323) is the place to go to find out all about dinosaurs. You'll also find the smallest mammal in the world there – the pygmy white-toothed shrew – and the largest, the Blue Whale! You can see how a space rocket works in the Science Museum (Exhibition Road, SW7 Tel: 01-589 3456), and look at all sorts of strange musical instruments – including a Sennet, used by rich ladies to teach their singing birds new tunes – at the Musical Instruments Gallery in the Victoria and Albert Museum (Cromwell Road, SW7 Tel: 01-589 6371). There's lots to see, and it's lots of fun!

To spot A little arcade outside the station. Look up to the roof and you'll see little lamps. The name of the station is written in the ironwork at both ends.

Sloane Square

To know The station was opened on 24th December 1868 but was severely damaged during bombings in World War II. It was rebuilt after the war and reopened in May 1951. One part of the station that wasn't hit by bombs was the square iron conduit above the platforms which, believe it or not, contains a river! It's the River Westbourne which eventually leads into the Thames.

To see You might see a Chelsea Pensioner – dressed in a scarlet velvet frock coat with a black tricorn hat – because you're very near Chelsea Royal Hospital (Royal Hospital Road, SW3) which is the home for Chelsea Pensioners who are retired soldiers. The Chelsea Flower Show is held in the grounds of the hospital every spring. There's a little museum here – look out for the portrait of a soldier called William Hiseland who lived to be 112! Still on an army theme, nearby is the National Army Museum (Royal Hospital Road, SW3 Tel: 01-730 0717). This shows you the story of the British Army from 1480. There are all sorts of weapons, paintings and medals. If you push a button you'll even hear some soldiers' songs!

To spot The decorations on the walls of the platform which make it look like a garden.

Victoria

To know The station was named in honour of Queen Victoria. The main line station was opened on 1st October 1860. The District Line underground station was opened on 24th December 1868. The Victoria Line platforms below it were opened on 7th March 1969.

To see Have you seen the Queen riding in a beautiful coach on television? Well, you can have a good goggle at all the elaborate state coaches, including the golden coronation coach, at The Royal Mews (Buckingham Palace Road, SW1) open on Wednesday and Thursday afternoons, 2.00 P.M. to 4.00 P.M. They're really like something from a fairy tale.

To spot A cameo of Queen Victoria's head in the tiles on the Victoria Line platform.

St James's Park

To know In 1532 King Henry VIII ordered this area, which was then very swampy, to be drained. He had it stocked with deer and it became one of his favourite hunting grounds. The station was opened on 25th December 1868.

To see St James's Park (The Mall, SW1) is the prettiest of all central London parks. Stand on the bridge over its lake and you can see both Buckingham Palace and the domes of Whitehall. There are all sorts of ducks, hungrily gobbling up bits of bread on the lake and if you want to know more about them there are helpful plaques outside the cafeteria. But it's the majestic pelicans with their enormous bills, which attract most attention.

To spot The unusual keystones, with decorative carved heads, on many of the buildings in Queen Anne's Gate, outside St James's tube station. How many different designs can you count? The building above St James's Park station is the headquarters of the London Underground. How many carved statues can you spot on the outside of the building? Walk all the way round!

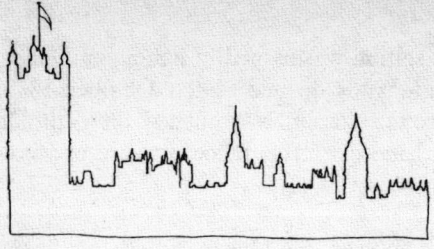

Westminster

To know Opened as Westminster Bridge on 24th December 1868, the station was renamed Westminster in 1907.

To see There's so much to see in the Westminster area that you could easily spend a whole day here. As you leave the station, you will see directly opposite you the world famous clock known as Big Ben (Palace of Westminster, SW1). But 'Big Ben' is actually the name of the huge bell, which weighs over 13 tons, inside the gilded tower you can see. Big Ben stands next to the Houses of Parliament (Palace of Westminster, SW1 Tel: 01-219 3000). It's possible, from seats in the Visitors Gallery, to watch politicians debate – but you may have to queue for a long time to get a place. Opposite the Houses of Parliament is the small church of St Margaret's (St Margaret Street, SW1). This is the parish church of the House of Commons and it's full of tradition. The headless body of Sir Walter Raleigh is said to be buried under its high altar. St Margaret's is dwarfed by enormous Westminster Abbey (Parliament Square, SW1 Tel: 01-222 5152) which looms over it. Founded in 1066, the Abbey has since been the setting for every coronation. You'll be able to see the tombs of many famous people including Queen Elizabeth I and William Shakespeare. From the Abbey walk up Whitehall to the cenotaph. This is a memorial to the people who died defending Britain in war. Nearby is 10 Downing Street, where the Prime Minister lives. Just round the corner are the Cabinet War Rooms (King Charles Street, SW1 Tel: 01-930 6961) where you can see the underground control rooms used by Winston Churchill and his staff during World War II.

To spot The jetty where Thames riverboat tours begin. You can spot them loading up with passengers. Or how about taking a trip yourself?

Embankment (see Bakerloo Line page 13)

Temple

To know The site of the nearby Law Courts and tube station was once owned by the Knights Templars. Their headquarters were near King Solomon's Temple in Jerusalem. They also called their headquarters in Paris and London 'Temple' – hence the name of the station! It was opened on 30th May 1870.

To see The Temple (Fleet Street, EC4), now the headquarters of London's lawyers. There are two areas – the Inner and Middle Temple. The hall of the Middle Temple is open for people to look around – it's really grand! Look at the serving table – that was made with timbers from Drake's ship, the 'Golden Hind'.

To spot The River Thames – you can't miss it!

Blackfriars

To know It's easy to work out where the name Blackfriars comes from – Black Friars! During the 13th century, a monastery was established here but was later closed down by King Henry VIII. Monks from the monastery wore long black habits and were known as 'black friars'.

The underground station was opened on 30th May 1870.

To see A short walk away is Fleet Street – the home of newspapers. How many clocks can you count as you walk its length? There really are a lot!

The Telecom Technology Showcase (135 Queen Victoria Street, EC4 Tel: 01-248 7444) tells you all about the history of telecommunications, from the first telegraph machine to fibre optics and satellite technology.

To spot From Blackfriars Bridge, the 'Oxo' tower across the water on the Thames south bank.

Mansion House

To know The station, which is named after the official residence of the Lord Mayor of London, was opened on 3rd July 1871.

To see Mansion House (EC4 Tel: 01-626 2500) is open for visits by groups on guided tours only, so you'll have to stand outside and try to imagine what it's like inside. Try to imagine too, what it was like here 300 years ago, before Mansion House was built – on the site of the old Stocks Market, where the Great Plague of 1665 started.

To spot St Mary Aldermary church. You can just see the top of it opposite the underground exit. Its entrance is in Bow Street, a narrow lane which leads to St Mary le Bow church (Cheapside, EC2). Do you remember singing 'Oranges and lemons'? Well, this is where the 'Great Bell of Bow' can be found. To be a true Cockney, a Londoner must be born within earshot of the 'Bow Bells'.

Cannon Street

To know The underground station was opened here on 6th October 1884. It is right underneath the main-line station, which was opened on 1st September 1866.

To see If you've studied any of William Shakespeare's plays at school you'll know they were performed in the Globe Theatre. You can see a reconstruction of the Globe in the Bear Gardens Museum (1, Bear Gardens, Bankside, SE1 Tel: 01-928 6342), just across the river.

To spot Number 80 Cannon Street; it's a really unusual piece of modern architecture which has much of its metal structure on the outside.

Monument

To know The station was called Eastcheap when it was opened on 6th October 1884, but was renamed Monument on 1st November

1884. The Monument-Bank (see page 33) subway opened on 18th September 1933.

To see The Monument (Monument Street, EC3 Tel: 01-626 2717) was put up to remind people of the horror of the Great Fire of London, 1666. The City blazed for days and some 13,200 houses and 87 churches were burnt. You can climb up the spiral staircase inside Monument – try counting how many steps there are. From the top there are fantastic views over the roof tops of London.

To spot Pudding Lane (EC3), where the Great Fire is said to have started in a baker's shop. To help you find it, it's exactly 202 feet (61.5 metres) from the base of Monument.

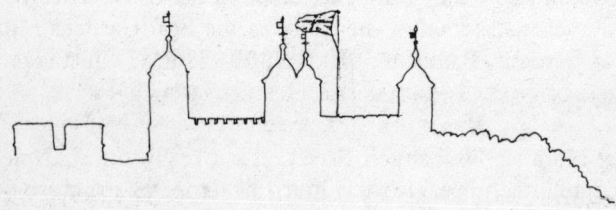

Tower Hill

To know The story of Tower Hill station is a little complicated. It was opened on 6th October 1884 as Mark Lane, but renamed Tower Hill on 1st September 1946. Then, on 5th February 1967, the station was resited to its present position which had been a station called Tower of London from 25th September 1882 until 12th October 1884. Phew!

To see A fortress, a palace, a royal residence, the Tower of London (Tower Hill, EC3 Tel: 01-709 0765) has been them all. It's now a very popular museum jam-packed with history. It was a prison for Walter Raleigh and Queen Elizabeth I (then a princess), and it was a place of execution for many people, including: Anne Boleyn,

Catherine Howard and Lady Jane Grey. Today it's guarded by Yeoman Warders popularly called Beefeaters!

To spot A statue of the Roman Emperor Trajan near the station.

Aldgate

To know Aldgate Station was first opened on 18th November 1876. It was reconstructed and reopened on 10th June 1926.

To see A stone bust of a gentleman called John Stow holding a real quill pen, in the church of St Andrew Undershaft (Leadenhall Street, EC3). Every year the Lord Mayor of London puts a new pen into his hand as part of an old church service which commemorates Stow's publication, in 1598, of a *Survey of London*.

Liverpool Street (see Central Line page 34)

Moorgate

To know Moorgate station, along with Baker Street (see page 16), has the largest number of platforms in the underground system – ten. It was opened as Moorgate Street in December 1865 and renamed Moorgate on 24th October 1924. In 1975, in a terrible fatal accident on the Northern Line, 43 people were killed at Moorgate.

To see The National Postal Museum (King Edward Building, King Edward Street, EC1 Tel: 01-432 3851) which has some 250,000 stamps in its collection, covering all the British issues from 1840 to the present day. So if you're a keen stamp collector, visit this museum and see how the experts do it!

If you've brought a packed lunch with you, Finsbury Circus Garden is a pretty place to munch it. Look out for a bandstand and an interesting sundial.

To spot On the corner of London Wall and Moorgate, a rectangular blue plaque which marks the site of the old Moor Gate, one of the gates of the old city, which was demolished in 1761.

Barbican

To know When it was opened on 23rd December 1865, this station was called Aldersgate. It was renamed Aldersgate and Barbican in 1923, but was renamed yet again on 1st December 1968 – this time simply Barbican.

To see The Barbican Centre (Barbican, EC2 Tel: 01-638 4141), opened in 1972 by the Queen, is a large arts complex. It took 130,000 cubic metres of concrete to build – that's the same amount as it takes to construct 19 miles of six-lane motorway! It's packed with things to see and do – theatres, exhibitions and films. There're often free concerts in the foyers and there's also a special children's cinema club.

Not far away is the Museum of London (150 London Wall, EC2 Tel: 01-600 3699). Here you'll find the Lord Mayor's coach, remains of Viking settlements, toys, costumes, musical instruments and much more. You can peep inside a Victorian shop and an air-raid shelter (try to imagine what it was like to sleep in such a shelter with bombs dropping outside). You can also see part of the original wall which once went all the way around the City of London.

If you like horses, visit the Whitbread Shire Stables (Garrett Street, EC1 Tel: 01-606 4455). These are real working horses which daily pull enormously heavy carts through the streets. You may even see a blacksmith at work fitting the horses with new shoes.

To spot A bright blue police box just outside the station.

Farringdon

To know Way back in 1279 a merchant of the City – William Farendon – was made an alderman. Farringdon Street (which was built in 1738 on arches over the river Fleet) was named after him and hence the name Farringdon for the station. This was the original City terminus of the Metropolitan Railway, the first underground railway in the world, opened on 10th January 1863.

To see Have you seen the St John Ambulance Brigade at work at some event, helping ill or injured people at perhaps a carnival or a football match? You can visit the Museum of the Order of St John (St John's Gate, St John's Lane, EC1 Tel: 01-253 6644) which shows their history. It's a very exciting history which is closely linked with the fortunes of the knights who went off on crusades in the Holy Land. Near the museum you can also visit Smithfield Market. It's the oldest wholesale market in Europe. Imagine, this busy market area was once, in the 17th century, an open space used for archery competitions!

To spot Outside Farringdon underground station there's a castle! Can you spot it?

King's Cross St Pancras

To know There are five lines running through King's Cross station – the Metropolitan Line, the Circle Line, the Piccadilly Line, the Northern Line and the Victoria Line. The first to be opened was the Metropolitan Line on 10th January 1863. The Victoria Line was added over a 100 years later and opened on 1st December 1968. Kings Cross St Pancras is the busiest station on the underground with about 65 million people starting and ending their journeys here every year.

To see You can spend hours train-spotting in Kings Cross and St Pancras stations – there's always something to watch. A short walk away from the stations is St Pancras Old Churchyard (Pancras Way NW1). It is worth going to see the amazing tomb of the architect Sir John Soane (see page 32). He designed it himself!

To spot Look up and up and up – the clock tower of St Pancras Station is 300 feet (91.4 metres) high!

Euston Square

To know Believe it or not, there was a farm on the site where the station now stands, as late as 1830. The station was opened on 10th January 1863 as Gower Street, then renamed Euston Square on 1st November 1909.

To spot Opposite the station, a huge office building with mirror glass. What can you see reflected in its windows?

Great Portland Street

To know The station was called Portland Road when it was first opened on 10th January 1963. It was renamed Great Portland Street on 1st March 1917.

To see This is one of the best stations for Regent's Park which always seems to be full of lovely flowers. There's a boating lake and plenty of places to play and watch different sports. During the summer, military bands hold concerts in the bandstand. Right in the centre of the park is Queen Mary's Garden – famous for its beautiful roses.

To spot A metal urn on a marble pedestal outside the station. It's used to grow bulbs now but see if you can find out why it's there.

Baker Street (see Bakerloo Line page 16)

Edgware Road

To know The station was opened on 10th January 1863. It serves the Circle, District and Metropolitan lines.

To see Seymour Leisure Centre (Bryanston Place, W1 Tel: 01-798 1421) is only a few minutes' walk away if you feel like going for a swim.

To spot Look at the Edgware Road (be careful though – it's very busy so cross by subway). This was once part of a road called Watling Street built by the Romans, which ran from Dover to St Albans.

DISTRICT LINE

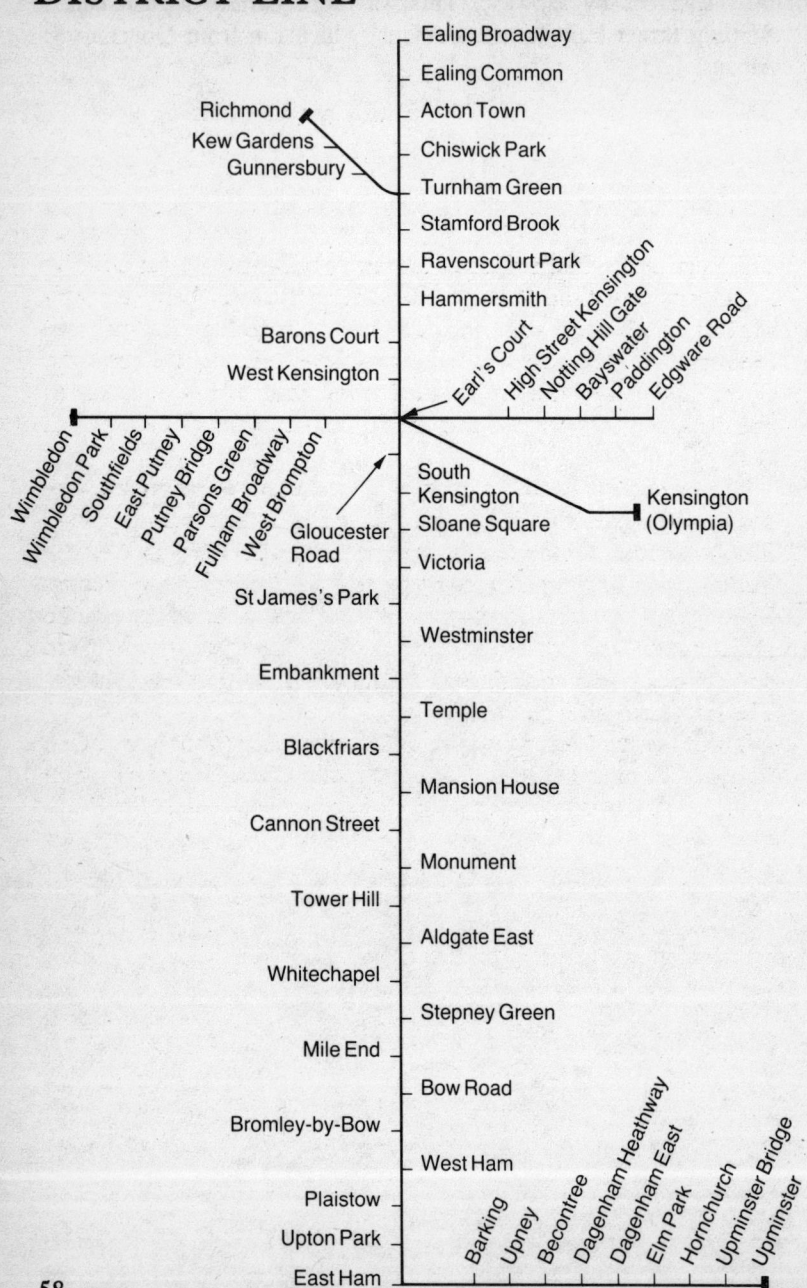

Ealing Broadway
Ealing Common
Acton Town
Chiswick Park
Turnham Green
Stamford Brook
Ravenscourt Park
Hammersmith

Richmond
Kew Gardens
Gunnersbury

Barons Court
West Kensington

Earl's Court
High Street Kensington
Notting Hill Gate
Bayswater
Paddington
Edgware Road

Wimbledon
Wimbledon Park
Southfields
East Putney
Putney Bridge
Parsons Green
Fulham Broadway
West Brompton

Gloucester Road

South Kensington
Sloane Square

Kensington (Olympia)

Victoria

St James's Park

Westminster

Embankment

Temple

Blackfriars

Mansion House

Cannon Street

Monument

Tower Hill

Aldgate East

Whitechapel

Stepney Green

Mile End

Bow Road

Bromley-by-Bow

West Ham

Plaistow

Upton Park

East Ham

Barking
Upney
Becontree
Dagenham Heathway
Dagenham East
Elm Park
Hornchurch
Upminster Bridge
Upminster

The story of the **District Line** is rather complicated. It was built by a company called the Metropolitan District Railway Company who worked with another company called the Metropolitan Railway (see Metropolitan Line page 84) to construct the 'Inner Circle' (now the Circle Line, page 42). Although they planned to join together as one company they fell out and so the District went its own way in 1871.

The company was rather poor so to try and get more money they started extending the line – to Hammersmith, Richmond, Ealing Broadway and Wimbledon. It was taken over in 1901 by Charles Yerkes, a wealthy American who formed the Underground Electric Railways of London Company and set about bringing all the underground lines, except the Metropolitan Line (see page 84) into one company and changing all the trains from steam to electric. The last steam train on the District Line ran in 1905.

The District Line now covers 40 route miles and stops at 60 stations. It runs between Upminster and Ealing Broadway with branches to Richmond, Wimbledon, Edgware Road and Olympia.

Edgware Road (see Circle Line page 56)

Paddington (see Bakerloo Line page 17)

Bayswater (see Circle Line page 44)

Notting Hill Gate (see Central Line page 28)

High Street Kensington (see Circle Line page 44)

Earl's Court

To know The station was first opened on 31st October 1871 but was burnt down on 30th December 1875 and repaired on a temporary

basis. A brand new station was built and opened on 1st February 1878.

The first escalator at an underground station was put in here in October 1911 (now there are around 273 escalators throughout the underground system!). People were a bit afraid of this new idea, so a man known as 'Bumper' Harris, who had a wooden leg, showed how safe it was by being the first person to use it.

To see The Earl's Court Exhibition Hall is right opposite the Warwick Road entrance/exit. It covers 19 acres and the shows held here attract visitors from all over the world. On Sundays, there's a market in the car park.

To spot Feeling hungry? There's a little shop selling fresh fruit on the platform!

West Brompton

To know Can you imagine this area covered with bright, yellow, flowering broom? Well, that's what it looked like once. The area, and therefore the underground station, got its name from Broom Town – a common with lots of broom near to the town. The station was opened here on 12th April 1869.

To see Fulham Pools (Normand Park, Lillie Road, SW6 Tel: 01-736 5821) are really great swimming pools. There're different ones for different activities including a water slide, a wave machine and a diving pit.

Fulham Broadway

To know The underground station was opened here on 1st March 1880, when it was called Walham Green. It was renamed Fulham Broadway on 2nd March 1952.

To see A short walk away is the King's Road. Popular with trend setters and tourists, you can have lots of fun window shopping along the King's Road – it's crammed with very unusual clothes.

To spot The huge lights which illuminate Stamford Bridge Stadium, they tower high over the pitch and stalls.

Parsons Green

To know On 1st May 1880, the underground station was opened here.

Putney Bridge

To know On 1st March 1880 the underground station was opened here and called Putney Bridge and Fulham. But it was renamed Putney Bridge and Hurlingham on 1st September 1902. It had yet another name change in 1932 when it was given its present name – Putney Bridge.

To see Bishop's Park (entrance off Bishops Avenue, SW6), beside the Thames, is a lovely place to visit. In its grounds is Fulham Palace which has an interesting botanical garden.

To spot Make sure you take a look at the small boats moored beside the bridge. Nearby there's a traditional pottery kiln – you'll be able to recognise it by its unusual shape.

East Putney

To know The station was opened here on 3rd June 1889.

To spot The unusual decorations and kiosk in the station forecourt, which has just been redesigned.

Southfields

To know The station was opened here on 3rd June 1889.

To see Have you watched the Wimbledon lawn tennis championships on television? Or perhaps you've been lucky enough to actually see a match being played at Wimbledon. Well, the Wimbledon Lawn Tennis Museum (The All England Club, Church Road, SW19 Tel: 01-946 6131) has an exhibition which will tell you all about the history of the game.

To spot There are quite a number of tower blocks in this area. How many can you count?

Wimbledon Park

To know The station was opened on 3rd June 1889.

To see Wimbledon Park is often forgotten because its neighbour – Wimbledon Common (see below) – is so much bigger and better known. However, the park is pretty with a large lake and golf course.

Wimbledon

To know The main-line station was opened on 21st May 1838. District Railway underground trains began running on 3rd June 1889.

To see The Polka Children's Theatre (240 The Broadway, SW19 Tel: 01-543 4888) presents lots of shows for all ages. They also run workshops in drama, magic, puppet-making and stage make-up which you can join (telephone them to get details). And there's a super collection of toys and puppets on display. If you're hungry, the Polka Pantry has delicious food – served in a Victorian railway setting!

Wimbledon Common is up the hill from the station (turn right). It's a great place to walk, but do go with a group of friends and take care not to get lost. With a map you'll be able to find: Caesar's Camp, the Royal Wimbledon Golf Course, White Cottage, Thatched Cottage and a windmill.

Ealing Broadway (see Central Line page 25)

Ealing Common

To know Although the station was called Ealing Common when it was opened on 1st July 1879, it was renamed Ealing Common and West Acton in 1886, but reverted to Ealing Common on 1st March 1910.

To see Ealing Common is a great place to find conkers in the autumn!

To spot Look at the roof-lights in the booking hall; can you see the London Transport logo?

Acton Town

To know This station was originally called Mill Hill Park. It was opened by the District Railway on 1st July 1879 then was rebuilt and re-opened in February 1910. It was renamed Acton Town on 1st March 1910. In 1932 the station was rebuilt to take Piccadilly Line services as well.

To see Gunnersbury Park Museum (Gunnersbury Park, Pope Lane W3 Tel: 01-992 1612), which has lots of beautifully restored old coaches, and chariots and other vehicles once used by the Rothschild family. Look out for the bath chair used by Baroness de Rothschild – it's much grander than travelling by the tube!

To spot The sign to Bollo Lane. Try to find out how it got its name.

Chiswick Park

To know This station has changed names three times. It was called Acton Green when it was first opened in July 1879, then renamed Chiswick Park and Acton Green in March 1887, and finally, just Chiswick Park on 1st March 1910! The present station was built in 1932.

Chiswick gets its name from the old English words 'cese' – cheese, and 'wic' – dairy farm. There used to be a cheese and dairy farm nearby.

To see A mile away is Chiswick House (Burlington Lane, W4 Tel: 01-995 0508), which was built in 1730. This was where all the leading thinkers, writers and artists used to meet. You can look around all the rooms but, best of all, are the lovely gardens with lots of different areas to explore.

To spot Not a dairy farm but a very large supermarket!

Richmond

To know The first main-line station here was opened by the London and South Western Railway on 27th July 1846. It was rebuilt in 1869 and first used by underground trains on 1st June 1877. The present station was built in 1938.

To see Richmond Park is full of red and fallow deer – and most of them are quite tame. You can fly your model aeroplane (or watch others!) at the Sheen Cross Roads in the park, or feed the ducks on Pen Ponds. There are lots of places to explore – but remember the park is very big, so don't get lost! Richmond Baths (Old Deer Park, Richmond Tel: 01-940 8461) have got a fantastic water shute, and there's an ice rink too – in fact, a very famous one. Richmond Ice Rink (Clevedon Road, Twickenham Tel: 01-892 3646) is where top skaters often come to practise or give coaching. You can hire skates here – so get skating!

To spot Two flags flying above the station – what are they?

Kew Gardens

To know The main line station was opened on 1st January 1869 and was first used by underground trains on 1st June 1877.

To see Follow the signs to Kew Gardens – or to give them their correct title, The Royal Botanic Gardens. There are thousands and thousands of different varieties and species of plants growing here. Look out for the Great Pagoda, a really tall Chinese style building, and the Palm House which has palm trees from all over the world. You can also see inside Kew Palace which was built in 1631 and lived in later by George III; and Queen Charlotte's Cottage where Queen Charlotte used to have an afternoon picnic.

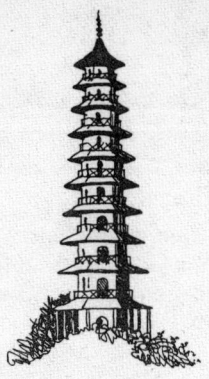

To spot A little concrete footbridge just outside the station. It's painted on both sides.

Gunnersbury

To know The station was opened by the London and South Western Railway on 1st January 1869 as a main-line station. It was renamed Gunnersbury on 1st November 1871. The first underground trains started using the station on 1st June 1877.

To see The world's largest steam pumping engines are at the Living Steam Museum (Kew Bridge Pumping Station, Kew Bridge Road, Brentford, Middx Tel: 01-568 4757), a 15 minute walk from the station. It's best to go at the weekend when you can see the engines working. There are special 'Steam Events' throughout the year.

Syon Park is near Gunnersbury station too. The house is open for people to look around, but the grounds are much more fun, especially the London Butterfly House (Tel: 01-560 0881) with its colourful butterflies and fantastic creepy-crawlies; and the British Heritage Motor Museum (Tel: 01-560 1378), a wonderful collection of British cars from the very earliest to the most modern.

To spot You've come by underground train but if you stand on the platform, you're in the car park!

Turnham Green

To know The station was first used by underground trains on 1st June 1877, although it had been used by the London and South Western Railway since 1st January 1869. The station was rebuilt and reopened on 3rd December 1911.

To see Hogarth was a very famous painter. He lived quite near here for 15 years. You can see some of his paintings at Hogarth's House (Hogarth Lane, Great West Road, Chiswick, W4 Tel: 01-994 6757). There's a sign outside the station to direct you.

To spot A drinking fountain on the corner of the green. Turn left out of the station then cross over the Zebra crossing.

Stamford Brook

To know The station was opened on 1st February 1912.

To spot You're near Ravenscourt Park so, as you might expect, there's a raven nearby – at least a picture of one!

Ravenscourt Park

To know The station was opened by the London and South Western Railway on 1st April 1873 and named Shaftesbury Road. It was first used by underground trains on 1st June 1877 and renamed Ravenscourt Park in 1888.

To see Ravenscourt Park is a fun place to visit with a play area and lots of sports pitches. It once belonged to Thomas Corbett, Secretary to the Admiralty, who had a raven in his coat of arms – and that's why it's called Ravenscourt Park.

To spot Stand on the eastbound platform and look to your left – a church spire stands out on the skyline.

Hammersmith

To know There are two stations at Hammersmith, connected by subways. The Metropolitan Line station was the first to open – on 13th June 1864. The District Line station was opened on 9th September 1874. Unfortunately, it was burnt down on 20th January 1882 but reopened on 23rd August 1882. The station was rebuilt to take Piccadilly Line trains as well from 15th December 1906, and partly rebuilt again in 1932.

To see There are two theatres nearby which both have special shows, workshops and events for young people – The Lyric Theatre (King Street, Hammersmith, W6 Tel: 01-741 2311), and Riverside Studios (Crisp Road, Hammersmith W6 Tel: 01-748 3354). It's best to visit on Saturdays or telephone beforehand to find out what's going on.

To spot The entrances to the subways have colourful iron arches. Can you count how many there are – to help you, there's a map outside each entrance!

Barons Court

To know It was opened on 9th October 1905 for District Line trains. The Piccadilly service started a year later on 15th December 1906.

To spot A cemetery gate. As you come out of the station turn to your right then right again and you're in Margravine Gardens. Just a little way along there's a gate leading to the cemetery. The greenery on the stonework makes it look like two curly heads, or maybe two beefeaters standing guard outside the entrance!

West Kensington

To know When the station was opened on 9th September 1874 it was known as North End (Fulham) but named West Kensington on 1st March 1877.

To spot Walk along West Cromwell Road and stand on the bridge. If you look towards the enormous Earl's Court Exhibition Hall you'll get a really good view of the criss-crossing underground railway tracks. It looks like a real maze!

Earl's Court (see page 60)

Kensington (Olympia)

To know A station called Kensington was opened here by the West London Railway on 27th May 1844. A new station was opened in 1863 and renamed Addison Road in 1868. It was first used by underground trains on 1st July 1864. The station was renamed Kensington (Olympia) in 1948.

To spot Olympia is an enormous exhibition hall – in fact, it covers 500,000 square feet! It's used for shows and exhibitions throughout the year. One of the very first shows held here was a circus called 'The Paris Hippodrome'. It was in 1886 and there were around 400 performing animals and a chariot race.

Gloucester Road (see Circle Line page 44)

South Kensington (see Circle Line page 45)

Sloane Square (see Circle Line page 46)

Victoria (see Circle Line page 47)

St James's Park (see Circle Line page 47)

Westminster (see Circle Line page 48)

Embankment (see Bakerloo Line page 13)

Temple (see Circle Line page 49)

Blackfriars (see Circle Line page 49)

Mansion House (see Circle Line page 50)

Cannon Street (see Circle Line page 51)

Monument (see Circle Line page 51)

Tower Hill (see Circle Line page 52)

Aldgate East

To know The first Aldgate East station was opened on 6th October 1884. It was then resited a little further east and reopened on 31st October 1938.

To see Petticoat Lane (off Middlesex Street, E1) is London's biggest market. You name it, you can buy it here. Best of all there are shops which sell delicious hot doughnuts and apple fritters – so this is one time *not* to take a packed lunch!

The Whitechapel Art Gallery (80 Whitechapel High Street, E1 Tel: 01-377 0107) has exhibitions of modern art. They change often so take a look and see what's on.

Whitechapel

To know Whitechapel underground station takes its name from the Chapel of St Mary Matfelon which was built from white stone. But don't try to look for it now, it was demolished in 1952! The East London Line station was opened on 10th April 1876 and the upper level District Line platforms from 1st October 1884.

Stepney Green

To know The station was opened on 23rd June 1902.

To see Stepping Stones Farm (Stepney Way, E1 Tel: 01-790 8204), is a real farm in the heart of the capital city. You can see just how a farm works – how fruit is grown and animals kept. You could even offer to help a little, and perhaps do some hoeing!

Mile End (see Central Line page 35)

Bow Road

To know This red brick station, which was opened on 11th June 1902, is listed by the Department of the Environment which means that it's thought to be very special and cannot be altered or demolished without permission.

To spot Red and white candy-striped pillars supporting the roof over the platform – you don't even have to get off the train to see them!

Bromley-by-Bow

To know The station here was opened on 2nd June 1902, but it was only named Bromley-by-Bow on 5th May 1968.

To see The Tide Mill in Three Mills Lane, E3, built in 1776. The mill wheels were driven by water from Bow Creek which runs underneath it.

To spot A large observation mirror at the end of the platform. By looking into it, the train driver can see all the way back down the platform.

West Ham

To know A station was first opened at West Ham on 1st February 1901 by the London, Tilbury and Southend Railway. It was first used by underground trains on 2nd June 1902 and was renamed West Ham Manor Road on 11th February 1924. However, it was shortened back to West Ham on 1st January 1969.

To spot Stratford Works, an immense chemical factory near the station.

Plaistow

To know A station was opened by the London, Tilbury and Southend Railway on 31st March 1858. It was first used by underground trains on 2nd June 1902.

To spot The Volkswagen-Audi Centre.

Upton Park

To know The station, which was first used by underground trains on 2nd June 1902, was opened in 1877 by the London, Tilbury and Southend Railway.

To see If you're a soccer fan, you can watch a match at the West Ham United Football Ground.

East Ham

To know On 31st March 1858, the station was opened by the London, Tilbury and Southend Railway. It was first used by underground trains on 2nd June 1902.

To spot The decorative ironwork of the platform roofing. It is really beautiful and if you try to draw its design you'll soon discover how complicated it is.

Barking

To know Underground trains first used this station on 2nd June 1902. It was first opened as a main-line station by the London, Tilbury and Southend Railway on 13th April 1854.

To spot The iron girders which support the platform roof have a pattern which is a particular six-sided shape. What is it?

Upney

To know The station was opened here on 12th September 1932.

Becontree

To know Opened as a railway station called Gate Street, Becontree was renamed and first used by underground trains on 12th September 1932.

Dagenham Heathway

To know The 'heathway' gets its name from the road which runs north through Dagenham and Becontree. The station was called Heathway when it was opened on 12th September 1932 but was renamed Dagenham Heathway in 1949.

Dagenham East

To know The London Tilbury and Southend Railway opened the station on 1st May 1885, calling it Dagenham. It was first used by underground trains on 2nd June 1902 and was renamed Dagenham East on 1st May 1949.

To see Nearby is the Dagenham Plant – the factory where Ford Motors are made.

To spot British Rail trains whizz past on a line parallel to the underground line. You can do some train spotting from the westbound underground platform.

Elm Park

To know Many years ago this area, which was then covered with Elm woods, was a favourite meeting place for local people. The station was opened here on 13th May 1935.

Hornchurch

To know The station was opened on 1st May 1885 by the London, Tilbury and Southend Railway. It was first used by underground trains on 2nd June 1902.

To see The church here dates from 1602. Inside there's a bull's head with horns!

Upminster Bridge

To know The station was opened on 17th December 1934.

Upminster

To know Upminster is about 18 miles from central London. The station which was opened by the London, Tilbury and Southend Railway was first used by underground trains on 2nd June 1902.

JUBILEE LINE

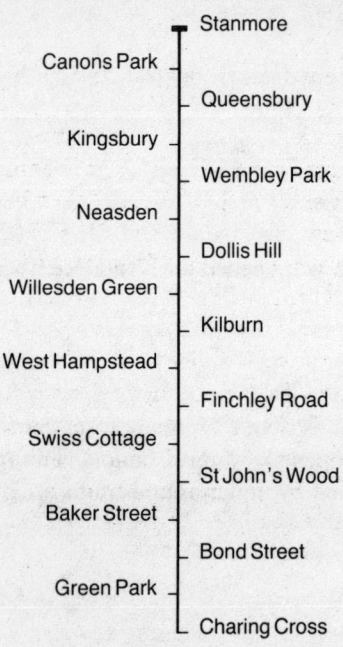

Stanmore
Canons Park
Queensbury
Kingsbury
Wembley Park
Neasden
Dollis Hill
Willesden Green
Kilburn
West Hampstead
Finchley Road
Swiss Cottage
St John's Wood
Baker Street
Bond Street
Green Park
Charing Cross

The **Jubilee Line** runs from Charing Cross to Stanmore. Its route is 14 miles long and it stops at 17 stations. Work began in 1972 with the hope that this new line, then called the Fleet Line, would take some of the traffic away from the Bakerloo Line between Baker Street and Oxford Circus. This section of the underground was getting really over-crowded with as many as 24,000 passengers travelling every hour at peak times.

Although called the Fleet Line in the early years, it changed its name to Jubilee in 1977 when the Queen was celebrating her Jubilee Year. It was finally completed in April 1979 and given a royal opening by the Prince of Wales. The first trains started running on 1st May 1979, taking over the Stanmore branch of the Bakerloo Line north of Baker Street.

Charing Cross (see Bakerloo Line page 13)

Green Park

To know The Piccadilly Line station was opened on 15th December 1906 and called Dover Street. It was rebuilt and renamed Green Park on 18th September 1933. The Victoria Line platforms were opened on 7th March 1969 and the Jubilee Line platforms on 1st May 1979.

To see The first thing you see when you come out of the station is Green Park – which lives up to its name with lots of green, green grass and not many flowers. This used to be a fashionable place for the gentry to take walks but these days it's popular with everyone. You can get to Buckingham Palace (The Mall, SW1) through Green Park. If the Queen is in residence, you'll see the Royal Standard flying from the roof. Whether she's there or not, the ceremony of the Changing of the Queen's Guards still takes place in the front courtyard every day at 11.30 A.M. in the summer and every other day in the winter. Get there early for a good view.

To spot The sparkling lights of the famous Ritz Hotel.

Bond Street (see Central Line page 31)

Baker Street (see Bakerloo Line page 16)

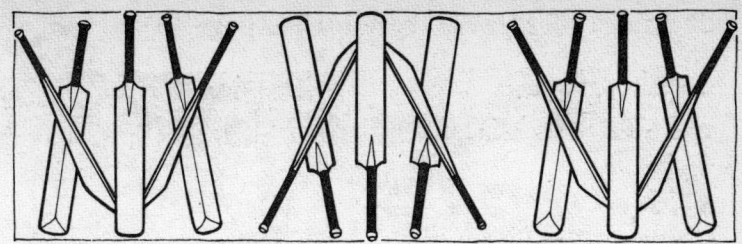

St John's Wood

To know The original Metropolitan Line station nearby was opened on 13th April 1868 but closed on 20th November 1939. The present station was opened on 20th November 1939. It was then part of the Bakerloo Line, but became part of the Jubilee Line in 1979.

To see Do you know how a cricket bat is made? What are the famous Ashes? You'll find out in the Cricket Memorial Gallery (Marylebone Cricket Club, Lord's Cricket Ground, NW8 Tel: 01-289 1611). It's a fascinating collection of trophies, pictures and everything to do with cricket. If you're a cricket fan, you might like to go on a tour of the cricket ground and around the pavilion. Ask an adult, perhaps your teacher, to contact the curator to arrange it for you.

To spot A portrait of Thomas Lord who founded Lord's Cricket Ground. Look closely at the tiles as you walk under the archways leading from the platform. This is one of the few tube stations that still has its bronze escalator lamps.

Swiss Cottage

To know A Metropolitan Line station was opened on 13th April 1868. However, when the new Bakerloo Line station opened here on 20th November 1939, the original Metropolitan platforms were closed. It became part of the Jubilee Line in 1979.

To see There's a great swimming pool just by the station. It's part of the Swiss Cottage Baths and Leisure Centre (Winchester Road,

NW3 Tel: 01-586 5989). Many sports go on here – from karate to basketball. You can take part or just watch.

To spot What else but Swiss Cottage itself – a very large 'pub' in London. It looks just like a Swiss chalet. An old toll-gate keeper's cottage used to stand on the site.

Finchley Road (see Metropolitan Line page 87)

West Hampstead

To know The station was opened for the Metropolitan Extension Line on 30th June 1879. It was rebuilt in 1939 when it became part of the Bakerloo Line and in 1979 joined the Jubilee Line.

To spot The main line station is just a little way from the underground station. If you walk to the bridge you can get a good view of the trains.

Kilburn

To know When the station was opened on 24th November 1879 by the Metropolitan Railway it was called Kilburn and Brondesbury.

It was rebuilt in 1939 to become part of the Bakerloo Line, and renamed Kilburn on 25th September 1950. It became part of the Jubilee Line in 1979.

To see Just a short walk down Kilburn High Road, you'll see a picture of a huge tricycle – this is the Tricycle Theatre (Tel: 01-328 8626) where you can not only see plays (some specially for young people) but take part in special workshops too and learn to act and mime.

To spot When you come out of the station, you're standing under three different bridges – do you know which railways run over them?

Willesden Green

To know The station was opened on 24th November 1879 by the Metropolitan Railway. It became a Bakerloo station in 1939 and Jubilee in 1979.

To see There's a swimming pool nearby at the Willesden Sports Centre (Donnington Road, NW10 Tel: 01-459 6605). Why not have a dip?

To spot The diamond-shaped clock outside the station. This was put up by the Metropolitan Railway when the station was rebuilt in 1925.

Dollis Hill

To know It was opened on 1st October 1909 by the Metropolitan Railway, rebuilt in 1939 for Bakerloo Line services and became a Jubilee Line station in 1979.

To spot The weather vane on top of Willesden College.

Neasden

To know The station was opened by the Metropolitan Railway on 2nd August 1880. At that time it was called Kingsbury and Neasden. It was renamed Neasden on 1st January 1932. It became a Bakerloo Line station in 1939 and Jubilee Line in 1979.

To see You can find out all about the history of the area at The Grange Museum (Neasden Lane, NW10 Tel: 01-452 8311). The museum is right in the middle of the busy Neasden Roundabout so you have to be careful and cross by the bridges – but you'll be glad you made it there! There are lots of different exhibits to show local life in the past and a special section all about the British Empire Exhibition held at Wembley in 1924 and 1925. Look out for the displays about London's railways!

To spot Can you see the twin towers of Wembley Stadium?

Wembley Park (see Metropolitan Line page 87)

Kingsbury

To know The station was opened on 10th December 1932 by the Metropolitan Railway. It became a Bakerloo Line station in 1939 and Jubilee Line in 1979.

To spot From the outside the station looks like a two-storey building, but don't be fooled! You'll spot the architectural trick when you're in the booking hall.

Queensbury

To know The station was opened on 16th December 1934 and called Queensbury for a very simple reason – a station called Kingsbury had been opened two years before and this was the next on the line! It was then a Metropolitan Line station. It became Bakerloo in 1939 and Jubilee in 1979.

To spot A roundabout opposite the station entrance. What do you think is in the centre?

Canons Park

To know The station was opened on 10th December 1932 by the Metropolitan Railway. It became a Bakerloo Line station in 1939 and Jubilee in 1979.

To spot A certificate by the booking office. Can you see what it was for?

Stanmore

To know The station was opened on 10th December 1932 by the Metropolitan Railway. It became a Bakerloo Line station in 1939 and Jubilee in 1979.

To spot This is the end of the Jubilee Line and if you follow the footpath from the station to the car park you can see the trains lined up ready to go out.

METROPOLITAN LINE

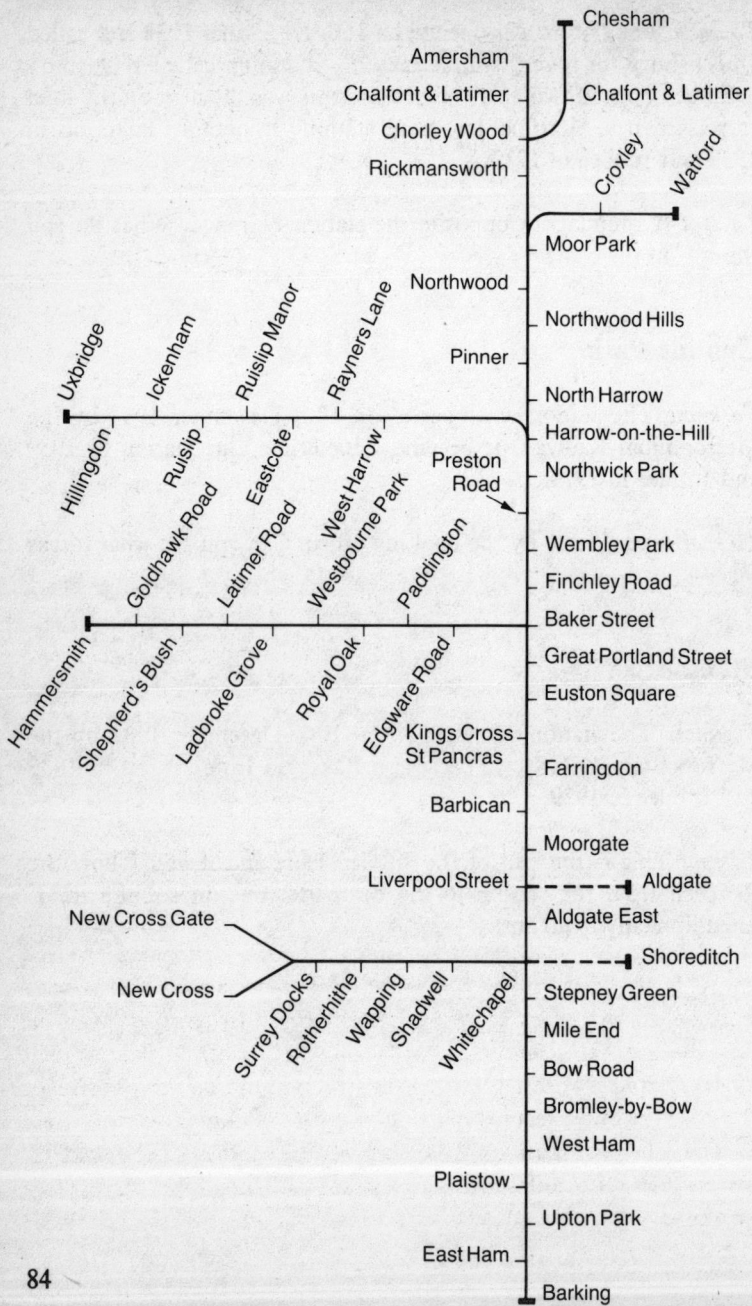

It was a great day in the history of transport when the **Metropolitan Line** was opened on 10th January 1863. This was the very first time anywhere in the world that passengers had travelled by underground railway. It was the idea of a man called Charles Pearson who thought it would be the best way of coping with all the traffic jams in London. A new company called the Metropolitan Railway Company was set up and building work began. The first section – which was nearly four miles long – ran between Paddington and Farringdon Street. Mr Gladstone rode in the first coach on the first ever journey which took 33 minutes.

People were rather rude about it at first – they called it the 'Drain', but it soon became a huge success. The trains were all steam-operated and had carriages for people paying first, second and third class fares. The Metropolitan Line soon extended to Hammersmith and Moorgate and plans were made to form an 'Inner Circle'. This circle (now known as the Circle Line see page 42), was finally completed in 1884. As more companies started building underground railways the traffic got heavier and it soon became difficult to run steam-operated trains. In January 1905, the first electric trains ran on the Metropolitan Line from Baker Street to Uxbridge. The last passenger steam train ran on 9th September 1961 on the outer section of the line beyond Rickmansworth.

The Metropolitan Line is the longest line on the underground. It covers 55 route miles and stops at 61 stations. There are three sections:

1 The main section runs from Baker Street (Aldgate in peak hours) to Amersham, with branches to Chesham, Watford and Uxbridge.

2 The Hammersmith and City Line runs from Hammersmith to Whitechapel with an extension to Barking in peak hours.

3 The East London section runs from Whitechapel (Shoreditch in peak hours) to New Cross or New Cross Gate.

Baker Street (see Bakerloo Line page 16)

Finchley Road

To know The station was opened on 30th June 1879 and rebuilt in 1939. An automatic barrier – the first ever – was installed in the car park here on 20th July 1964.

To spot A very modern church opposite the station. Can you find out its name?

Wembley Park

To know The station was opened on 12th May 1894 but has been rebuilt and enlarged since. Its busiest time was during the Olympic Games of 1948 when 433,000 spectators came to Wembley by underground. During those 15 days, over a million people used Wembley Park Station! It's still very busy today – it's got the biggest car park of all the underground stations with 634 car spaces.

To see Here's your chance to see behind the scenes at Wembley Stadium, and even try on an England 'cap'. There are guided tours of Wembley nearly every day – and you can join one. As well as seeing all around the stadium you'll also be shown a film about its history right from the very first FA Cup Final ever played here in 1923. Do you know which teams were playing?

To spot A stone plaque in the wall outside the station with the letters M.R. They stand for 'Metropolitan Railway'.

Preston Road

To know The station was a halt when it was first opened on 21st May 1908, but was resited to its present position on the Metropolitan Line on 22nd November 1931.

To spot A little ornate window in the building above the station entrance.

Northwick Park

To know The station was opened as Northwick Park and Kenton on 28th June 1913. It was renamed Northwick Park on 15th March 1937.

To spot Can you see Northwick Park Hospital?

Harrow-on-the-Hill

To know When the station was opened on 2nd August 1880, it was called Harrow. It was given the name Harrow-on-the-Hill on 1st June 1894. The station was rebuilt in the 1940s.

To see Harrow is best known for its famous Harrow School. Sir Winston Churchill was a pupil here, so too were other well known people such as Sir Robert Peel, Cardinal Manning and Lord Byron. If you arrange to go on a special tour, you can still see the old school-room where they used to study, and the punishment stool where they were whipped for being naughty. Why not ask an adult, perhaps your teacher, to arrange for you to look around the school. You should write or telephone: Tours Organiser, Harrow School, 15 London Road, Harrow-on-the-Hill, Middx HA1 3JJ Tel: 01-422 2303.

To spot A lovely little park just outside the station entrance.

North Harrow

To know The station was opened on 22nd March 1915. Beware, it's said to be haunted!

To spot You can still see the very top of the old railway bridge sticking through on the railway track.

Pinner

To know The station was opened here on 25th May 1885.

Northwood Hills

To know The station was opened on 13th November 1933.

Northwood

To know The station was opened on 1st September 1887.

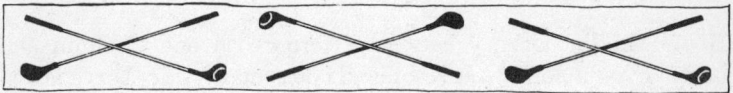

Moor Park

To know Moor Park is a famous golf course. On 9th May 1910, the underground station was opened and called Sandy Lodge. It was renamed Moor Park and Sandy Lodge on 18th October 1923, then on 25th September 1950 it was shortened to simply Moor Park.

To spot Outside the station there's a little stream running through the park.

Rickmansworth

To know The station was opened on 1st September 1889.

To spot There's some unusual, bright red metal girders supporting the roof of the platform – a big contrast to the rest of this 19th century station.

Chorleywood

To know The station was opened on 18th July 1889.

To see Definitely well outside central London – just look at all the fields and woods to explore around here.

To spot Like most of the stations at this end of the Metropolitan Line, Chorleywood has some interesting decorative ironwork supporting its platform roof.

Chalfont and Latimer

To know On 8th July 1889, the station was opened and called Chalfont Road. It was renamed Chalfont and Latimer in 1915.

To see On the journey between Chorleywood and Chalfont and Latimer you'll notice you've entered open countryside. Large fields, lots of trees and no buildings! It's a lovely area to visit and to do some walking in.

To spot A building with a bright blue roof. What is it?

Amersham

To know About 27 miles from central London, the station here at Amersham was opened on 1st September 1892. It's about 500 feet (150 metres) above sea level.

To spot Amersham is one of the stations used by commuters who leave their cars in the station car park and travel to work by train. How many cars can you count?

Chesham

To know The station was opened on 8th July 1889.

Croxley

To know Opened as Croxley Green on 2nd November 1925, the station was renamed Croxley on 23rd May 1949.

Watford

To know The station was opened on 2nd November 1925.

To see Near to this station is Cassiobury Park, through which runs a stretch of the Grand Union Canal, with a lock and a leafy tow path and a river with watercress beds.

Great Portland Street (see Circle Line page 56)

Euston Square (see Circle Line page 56)

Kings Cross St Pancras (see Circle Line page 55)

Farringdon (see Circle Line page 54)

Barbican (see Circle Line page 54)

Moorgate (see Circle Line page 53)

Liverpool Street (see Central Line page 34)

Aldgate (see Central Line page 53)

Aldgate East (see District Line page 70)

Whitechapel (see District Line page 71)

Stepney Green (see District Line page 71)

Mile End (see Central Line page 35)

Bow Road (see District Line page 71)

Bromley-by-Bow (see District Line page 72)

West Ham (see District Line page 72)

Plaistow (see District Line page 72)

Upton Park (see District Line page 73)

East Ham (see District Line page 73)

Barking (see District Line page 73)

West Harrow

To know It was opened on 17th November 1913.

To spot A little tree-lined path leading up to the station. Can you count the steps?

Rayners Lane

To know There's a story that an old farmer called Rayner lived in a cottage here in Victorian times and that's how the area got its name. The station was opened in May 1906.

To spot The cinema just down the road (turn right) is a very odd shape. What does it remind you of?

Eastcote

To know It was opened on 26th May 1906.

Ruislip Manor

To know The station was opened on 5th August 1912.

To see You're out in the country here. There are some very pretty walks along the River Pinn.

Ruislip

To know The station was opened on 4th July 1904.

To see Spending a day at Ruislip Lido (Reservoir Road, Ruislip Tel: 0895 63481) is just like being by the seaside – there's a sandy beach, a miniature railway and crazy golf and, of course, an open-air pool. There are lots of woods around and places to explore.

Ickenham

To know The station was opened on 25th September 1905. The area around the station was mentioned in the Domesday Book as 'Ticheha'.

Hillingdon

To know The station was opened on 10th December 1923.

To see This is the place to go to see skiers practicing – or even have a go yourself. There's a dry ski slope at Hillingdon Ski Centre (Park Road, Uxbridge, Middx Tel: 0895 55183). It's not the same as the real thing, of course, but still good fun.

To spot Northolt Airport is very near – you can see the planes arriving and leaving.

Uxbridge

To know The original Metropolitan Railway station was opened nearby on 4th July 1904. A new station was opened on the present site on 4th December 1938.

To see Although you can't actually go in, you can look at RAF Uxbridge from the outside. From here Winston Churchill directed the Battle of Britain in 1940 and here he said those famous words: 'Never in the field of human conflict was so much owed by so many to so few.' The legendary Lawrence of Arabia served at RAF Uxbridge in 1922.

To spot Stained glass windows in the station showing three coats of arms. What do they represent? Ask in the local library (turn left outside the station).

Edgware Road (see Circle Line page 56)

Paddington (see Bakerloo Line page 17)

Royal Oak

To know The station was opened on 30th October 1871. It takes its name from an old railway tavern which could only be reached by a wooden plank over the Westbourne River.

To spot Stand on the eastbound platform (not too near the edge) and you can see the underground trains as they leave Westbourne Park then disappear down the tunnel and reappear again. It's like a magic act! You also get a good view of the main-line trains coming out of Paddington.

Westbourne Park

To know It was opened on 1st February 1866.

To spot The pretty coloured poles on the station platform. It looks like May Day.

Ladbroke Grove

To know When the station was opened on 13th June 1864 it was known as Notting Hill. It changed names twice again before becoming Ladbroke Grove in 1938.

To see Portobello Road (you'll see signs at the station) is one of London's liveliest markets – people come from all over the country to rummage through the antiques and bric-à-brac for sale. The best time to come is on Saturday. It does get very crowded so hang onto your purse, and your friend!

To spot The cars hurtling past on the motorway which runs beside the station.

Latimer Road

To know The station was opened on 16th December 1868.

To spot Look out for the pig playing a whistle!

Shepherd's Bush (Metropolitan Line)

To know The station was first opened on 13th June 1864, but resited and reopened on 1st April 1914.

To see Right under the railway viaduct is Shepherd's Bush Market which has all sorts of interesting things for sale. There are some very strange looking vegetables on the stalls. Try to find out their names. During the war these railways arches where the market is now were used for billeting troops and stabling horses.

To spot The bright and colourful sign in front of Shepherd's Bush market.

Goldhawk Road

To know It was opened on 1st April 1914.

To spot The railway bridge, painted in lovely bright colours – red, blue and yellow.

Hammersmith (see District Line page 68)

Shoreditch

To know Long ago, Shoreditch was a small village on an old Roman road. Well, that's all changed as you'll quickly see. The station was opened here on 10th April 1876.

Shadwell

To know Shadwell is a very ancient area which was mentioned in the Domesday Book in 1233. It's name means 'shallow well'. The station was opened here on 10th April 1876.

Wapping

To know When this station was opened on 7th December 1869 it was called Wapping and Shadwell but on 10th April 1876 it was renamed Wapping. Underground trains first used it on 1st October 1884. The tunnel between here and Rotherhithe was built between 1825 and 1843 by the great engineers Marc Isambard Brunel and his son Isambard Kingdom Brunel. This was the first tunnel under the Thames. At first it was only used by pedestrians, but a railway was laid through it in 1869.

To see If you're interested in sailing, make for St Katharine Docks (Tel: 01-481 0043). There are lots of modern boats moored here and an interesting lock system. And look out for the huge anchor.

To spot This is the prettiest part of the docklands to wander in. Many of the 19th century warehouses are now being converted into luxury homes – see if you can spot the sign for 'Gun Wharves and Warehouses'. Panels on the station platforms tell you about the building of the Thames Tunnel.

Rotherhithe

To know This is one of the original East London Railway stations – the outside looks just as it would have done when it was opened on 7th December 1869.

Surrey Docks

To know When the Surrey Docks opened in 1807 they were the centre of the timber trade. The station was opened on 7th December 1869 when it was called Deptford. It was first used by underground trains on 1st October 1884 and renamed Surrey Docks on 17th July 1911.

To spot Squat columns supporting the roofs of both the south and the northbound platforms. How many can you count?

New Cross

To know Try to imagine when you're here what it was like way back in 1648. There was Civil War in England and fierce fighting took place in the New Cross area.

The main-line station was opened by the South Eastern Railway in 1850. East London Line trains used a separate station next door from 7th December 1869 until 1876. Underground trains first used the station from 1st October 1884.

To see The Livesey Museum (682 Old Kent Road, SE15 Tel: 01-639 5604) has interesting exhibitions on a variety of subjects.

New Cross Gate

To know This station was first opened by the London and Croydon Railway on 5th June 1839. It was used by East London Line trains from 7th December 1869. The station was renamed New Cross Gate on 9th July 1923.

NORTHERN LINE

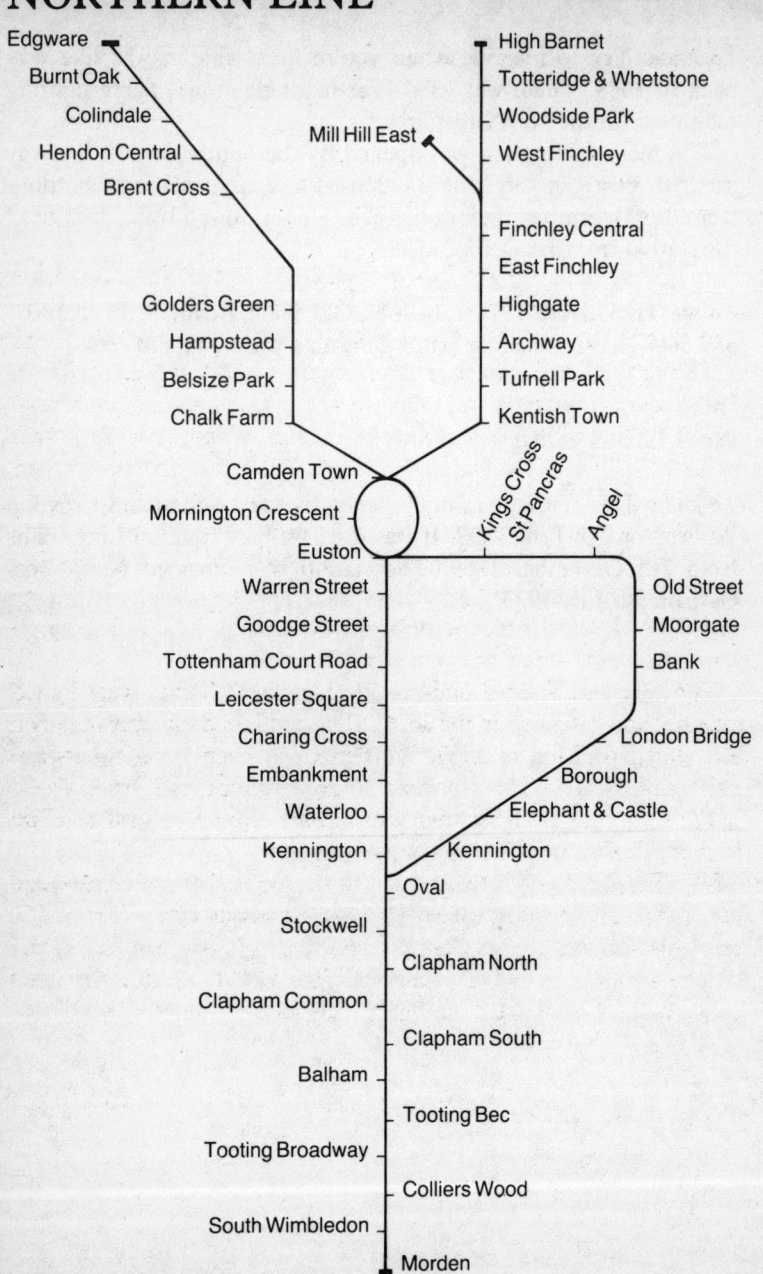

Edgware
Burnt Oak
Colindale
Hendon Central
Brent Cross

Mill Hill East

High Barnet
Totteridge & Whetstone
Woodside Park
West Finchley

Finchley Central
East Finchley

Golders Green
Hampstead
Belsize Park
Chalk Farm

Highgate
Archway
Tufnell Park
Kentish Town

Camden Town
Mornington Crescent
Euston

Kings Cross
St Pancras
Angel

Warren Street
Goodge Street
Tottenham Court Road
Leicester Square
Charing Cross
Embankment
Waterloo
Kennington

Old Street
Moorgate
Bank

London Bridge
Borough
Elephant & Castle
Kennington
Oval

Stockwell

Clapham North

Clapham Common

Clapham South

Balham

Tooting Bec

Tooting Broadway

Colliers Wood

South Wimbledon

Morden

The oldest section of the **Northern Line** was the first deep level underground electric tube railway in the world. It was called the City and South London Railway and opened between Stockwell and King William Street (near Monument) on 18th December 1890. The line was extended in 1900, south to Clapham Common and north to Moorgate, bypassing the original King William Street terminus to run via London Bridge and Bank. The line reached Euston in 1907.

A separate section of what became the Northern Line was also opened in 1907. This was known as the Hampstead Tube, running from Charing Cross to Camden Town, with branches to Highgate and Golders Green. It was officially opened by Lloyd George on 22nd June 1907 – and everyone was given a free ride!

The City and South London and Hampstead Tubes were joined together and extended in the 1920s. The combined line was renamed the Northern Line in 1937, and extended even further between 1939 and 1941. It now covers 36 route miles and stops at 50 stations. It runs from Morden to Edgware, Mill Hill East or High Barnet, via Bank or Charing Cross.

What makes the Northern Line so special is that the tunnels are very deep. The deepest is near Hampstead station where it runs 250 feet (76.2 metres) below Hampstead Heath. It also has one of the longest continuous railway tunnels in the world, 17.25 miles from East Finchley to Morden via Bank. Try riding through it!

Morden

To know Opened 13th September 1926, Morden is the most southerly tube station on the Northern line. It's approximately 10 miles from central London. The longest continuous tunnel in the underground system runs from Morden to East Finchley (see page 115) via Bank (see page 33), a distance of over 17 miles!

To spot A chandelier somewhere in the station.

South Wimbledon

To know The station was opened on 13th September 1926.

To spot A very unusual circular light fitting at the entrance to the station, near the ticket office. How many light bulbs is it studded with?

Collier's Wood

To know The station was opened on 9th September 1926.

Tooting Broadway

To know The station was opened on 9th September 1926. The 'Broadway' was once a very large open space. Now it's just a small triangle of land near the station.

To spot Edward VII watching over Tooting Broadway – well, his statue anyway!

Tooting Bec

To know Opened 13th September 1926, this station was originally called Trinity Road. It was renamed Tooting Bec 1st October 1950.

To see Tooting Bec Common is nearby. It has a pond and swimming pool, so remember to take your bathing costume.

To spot A picture of a sheaf of wheat . . . somewhere!

Balham

To know The station was opened on the 6th December 1926. It was badly damaged during the bombing of London in World War II.

To see Outside the station there's some ornate ironwork – around the entrance to the public loos! They are open from 7.00 A.M. until 10.30 P.M. – should you need them!

Clapham South

To know The station was opened 13th September 1926.

To see This is the nearest station to the south side of Clapham Common. You can fish in a pond on this side of the common or feed the ducks. There's also a recreation ground on the west side and nearer the centre is a colourful bandstand.

Clapham Common

To know Clapham is an ancient village which was mentioned in the Domesday Book. The tube station was opened here 3rd June 1900.

To see When you come out of the station you'll be able to see Clapham Common. It's a very popular and busy place with football pitches, a paddling pool, tennis courts, netball courts and a small café. If you have a kite this is a good place to fly it. On Sundays, during the summer, model power boats are raced on Long Pond. They're lots of fun to watch.

To spot Near the station a cattle trough which dates from the last century when sheep and cows were driven through here. Can you discover its date?

Clapham North

To know Originally opened as Clapham Road on 3rd June 1900, the station was renamed Clapham North on 13th September 1926.

To spot Whatever the weather, there always seems to be a flower seller standing outside the station. How many different types of flowers on sale can you name?

Stockwell

To know Until the 1860's, Stockwell was just a small rural village. But by 18th December 1890, when the station was opened, it was already beginning to grow. Today the station is totally surrounded by very busy roads. The station was rebuilt when the Victoria Line was opened on 23rd July 1971.

To spot Stockwell Bus Garage (turn left outside the station). You are not allowed inside but you can see its huge glass and concrete roof from the entrance. How many buses are inside?

Oval

To know The station was opened here on 18th December 1890.

To see A few minutes walk away is the London Taxi Museum (1–3 Brixton Road Tel: 01-735 7777). There're some 30,000 black taxi cabs in London and at the museum you'll be able to see how much their shape has changed. The earliest taxi on display dates from 1907. There's also the first cab to have an illuminated roof sign, and even an electric cab!

To spot Have you seen the distinctive shape of the Oval Cricket Ground on television? Well, it's just opposite the tube station. The first piece of turf was laid here in 1845 and the first Test Match was played in 1880 – England *v.* Australia.

Kennington

To know Opened on 18th December 1890, the underground station at Kennington is now a listed building which means it can't be altered or demolished without special permission from the Department of the Environment. It is protected because it is the only one of the original City and South London Railway tube stations which has not been rebuilt.

Elephant and Castle (see Bakerloo Line page 11)

Borough

To know The station was opened on 18th December 1890.

To see If you've ever read 'Little Dorrit' by Charles Dickens, you should visit the church of St George the Martyr, opposite the station. This is where Little Dorrit was found asleep on the steps and taken in for the night. There's a picture of her in the stained glass window.

Look up to the clock above the church. At one time only three of the four faces lit up at night so the people who lived in Bermondsey couldn't see the time. This was because they hadn't paid anything to the Church Appeal!

London Bridge

To know It's thought that there was probably a bridge over the Thames here 2,000 years ago. The present one was opened in March 1973 and cost four million pounds! The underground station was opened on 25th February 1900.

To see Not very many people seem to know about Southwark Cathedral (Cathedral Street, SE1) but it's a lovely place to visit. Look out for the memorial to William Shakespeare.

HMS Belfast (Symon's Wharf, Vine Lane, Tooley Street, SE1 Tel: 01-407 6434) is a wonderful ship to clamber over. You can go on board and explore its seven decks all you want.

To spot If you're very lucky you may see Tower Bridge lifted to allow a big ship to sail through – but that doesn't happen often.

From London Bridge you'll have an excellent view of Tower Bridge – the last bridge to span the Thames (from here on down the river becomes too wide to bridge).

Bank (see Central Line page 33)

Moorgate (see Circle Line page 53)

Old Street

To know The station was opened on 17th November 1901.

To see Bunhill Fields is a fascinating place to visit, so don't be put off because it's a burial ground! The name, Bunhill, comes from 'Bone Hill' – where victims of the Great Plague of 1665 were buried, some 100,000 bodies in all.

Angel

To know The station was opened on 17th September 1901.

To see If you're interested in the theatre there are two very different ones near here which are both well worth going to – the Sadler's Wells Theatre (Rosebery Avenue, EC1 Tel: 01-278 8916) and the Little Angel Marionette Theatre (14 Dagmar Passage, Cross Street, N1 Tel: 01-226 1787). Sadler's Wells is popular with visiting opera and ballet companies while the Little Angel is the only permanent marionette (puppets with strings) theatre in London.

To spot A picturesque clock outside the station.

Kings Cross St Pancras (see Circle Line page 55)

Waterloo (see Bakerloo Line page 12)

Embankment (see Bakerloo Line page 13)

Charing Cross (see Bakerloo Line page 13)

Leicester Square

To know The Piccadilly Line platforms were opened on 15th December 1906 and the Northern Line on 22nd June 1907. The escalators to the Piccadilly Line are the longest on the Underground, 161 feet 6 inches (49.6 metres). The vertical rise is 80 feet 9 inches (24.6 metres) and, comb-to-comb, they are about 175 feet (53.3 metres) long. The shortest distance between any two tube stations is the 0.16 miles between Leicester Square and Covent Garden (see page 124) on the Piccadilly Line.

To see The National Portrait Gallery (St Martins Place, WC2 Tel: 01-930 1552) is the place to go to see kings and queens, actors and politicians, painters and poets. They're all there – looking at you!

To spot A delightful little figure of Charlie Chaplin in Leicester Square.

Tottenham Court Road (see Central Line page 31)

Goodge Street

To know When it was opened on 22nd June 1907, this station was called Tottenham Court Road. It was renamed Goodge Street on 9th March 1908, the same day that Oxford Street station was renamed Tottenham Court Road.

To see Two small houses have been joined together to make the Pollock's Toy Museum (1 Scala Street, W1 Tel: 01-636 3452). It's crammed with all sorts of toys, mainly to do with the theatre, art or design. So, if you like toys, you'll like Pollock's!

To spot A large colourful wall mural next to the tube station, in Tottenham Street. Above it you can see the fantastically shaped Telecom Tower – 619 feet (188.7 metres) high!

Warren Street

To know When it was opened on 22nd June 1907, this station was called Euston Road. But on 7th June 1908 it was renamed Warren

Street. It was rebuilt in the 1930s. The Victoria Line platforms were opened on 1st December 1968.

To spot Capital Radio – it's actually only the bottom two floors of Euston Tower.

Euston

To know The City and South London tube station was opened on 12th May 1907 and the separate Hampstead Tube station on 22nd June 1907. These were linked together in 1924. The station was rebuilt again for the opening of the Victoria Line on 1st December 1968.

To see All the trains leaving from Euston main-line station are heading for the Midlands and beyond – look at the train information boards to see all the different destinations. There are 18 platforms – so it's a good place for train spotting.

To spot A statue of Robert Stephenson, engineer of the London to Birmingham railway line, on the station forecourt.

Mornington Crescent

To know The station was opened on 22nd June 1907 and has changed very little since then.

To spot Take a walk round Mornington Crescent. Blue plaques recording the many famous writers and artists who have lived here can be seen on the houses.

Camden Town

To know The station was opened on 22nd June 1907. Camden Town junction is the most complicated on the Underground. Four branches of the Northern Line meet here.

To see Bring your kite with you to Camden Town – you're near Parliament Hill Fields where all the biggest and best kites are flown. There are some ponds for sailing model boats too – but if you'd sooner go in a real boat, the 'Jenny Wren' will take you along the canal from Camden Lock to Little Venice and back (Tel: 01-485 4433 to find out times). And while you are at Camden Lock, look around the market – you can never be quite sure what's going to be on sale!

To spot The sign outside which says you're half-way there!

Chalk Farm

To know Your ride in the lift doesn't take very long at Chalk Farm – the station, which was opened on 22nd June 1907, has the shortest lift shaft on the underground, 30 feet 6 inches (9.3 metres).

To see Treat yourself to a yummy ice from Marine Ices, just opposite the station. They're probably the best in London!

To spot The Round House is just a little way along Chalk Farm Road. It was once the turning shed of the London and Birmingham Railway. It housed a turntable on which locomotives were turned round.

Belsize Park

To know Belsize Park station gets its name from a manor house and park which once stood here. It means 'beautifully situated' and some ten streets in this part of London are called Belsize. The underground station was opened on 22nd June 1907.

To see Hampstead Heath is just five minutes' walk away. It's a really great place to spend a whole day. There are ponds and lakes (you can even swim in one of them) and lots of open space.

To spot As you walk down to Hampstead Heath, look out for the Royal Free Hospital.

Hampstead

To know Hampstead station was opened on 22nd June 1907. Its lift shaft is the deepest of the underground system – 181 feet (55.2 metres). Perhaps you'd rather go by the stairs. There are 365 steps – count them!

To see Have you read any of Keats' poems in school? Well, you can visit the house he lived in. (Wentworth Place, Keats Grove, NW3 Tel: 01-435 2062.)

To spot The black and white lettering of the station name – Hampstead. This sort of lettering was a feature of all the stations on what was once known as the Hampstead Tube.

Golders Green

To know The station was opened on 22nd June 1907.

To see There's a part of Hampstead Heath called Golders Hill Park which is a wonderful place – with deer, wallabys, pheasants, rabbits, pygmy goats and sheep!

To spot You can't miss the Hippodrome – the largest building around. When it was opened in 1913 it was a famous music hall. Now it's a BBC studio.

Brent Cross

To know It was opened as Brent on 19th November 1923 but renamed Brent Cross on 20th July 1976.

To see Brent Cross Shopping Centre is one of the most popular shopping centres in London. There are all sorts of different shops under one roof. And if you get bored, there are some pretty fountains and very interesting seats!

To spot The pathway to the shopping centre goes up and down, round and about – it's fun following it!

Hendon Central

To know It was opened on 19th November 1923.

To see You can find out what life was like in the 17th, 18th and 19th centuries when Hendon was all farmland, in the Church Farm House Museum (Greyhound Hill, NW4 Tel: 01-203 0130). There's a park nearby too – Sunny Hill Park – which has tennis courts and a playground area. And not far away is the Copthall Pool and Sports Stadium (Great North Way, NW4 Tel: 01-203 4187), so take your swimming costume with you!

To spot Eight white stone pillars outside the entrance to the station.

Colindale

To know It was opened on 18th August 1924.

To see A very short walk away are two aircraft hangers from World War I. These are part of the Royal Air Force Museum (Tel: 01-205 2266) which traces the history of the RAF. There are lots of aeroplanes, including the Bleriot Monoplane of 1909, and models, uniforms, medals, flying aids and much more. Close by are the Battle of Britain Museum, devoted to 'The Few' who fought the famous Battle of Britain, and the Bomber Command Museum showing the history of bomber aircraft.

To spot The big building to your right, opposite the station entrance, is the Newspaper Library – it contains thousands and thousands of newspapers dating back to 1801.

Burnt Oak

To know The station was opened on 27th October 1924.

To spot Turn right out of the station and there's a tiny little alleyway leading down to Watling Market – a Saturday market.

Edgware

To know The station was opened on 18th August 1924.

To see You might be able to play a musical instrument, but have you any idea how one is made? You can find out all about the blowing, polishing and tuning at the Boosey & Hawkes factory (Deansbrook Road, Edgware, Middx Tel: 01-952 7711) if you go on a special tour. Ask an adult to arrange it. They've also got a collection of really old and rare instruments.

To spot Look to your left as you come out of the station onto the main road. Can you see the old hanging gibbet outside the black and white building?

Kentish Town

To know The station was opened on 22nd June 1907.

To see The name Kentish Town comes from a farm which used to be nearby, and although that farm's no longer here there is the Kentish Town City Farm (1 Cressfield Close, off Grafton Road, NW5 Tel: 01-482 2861) where you can see what life is like on a farm.

To spot The beautiful pointed turret of the old Assembly House to your right.

Tufnell Park

To know The station was opened on 22nd June 1907.

To spot Two pretty wrought-iron lamps outside the entrance.

Archway

To know The station was opened on 22nd June 1907 and called Highgate. It was renamed Archway (Highgate) on 11th June 1939 then Highgate (Archway) on 19th January 1941. It was finally called Archway in December 1947.

To see One of the most famous cemeteries in London is Highgate Cemetery which is just a short walk away. It's a really eerie place with catacombs, tombs and vaults. You can walk around the Eastern Cemetery on your own (look out for the grave of Karl Marx) but a guide will show you around the Western Cemetery (there's a guided tour every hour, on the hour). Ask to see the grave of Tom Sayers, the last of the barefist fighters.

To spot A stone with a black cat on top. It marks the spot where Dick Whittington is said to have heard the sound of the Bow Bells telling him to 'turn again' to London. Turn left out of the station into Highgate Hill.

Highgate

To know The station was first used by underground trains on 19th January 1941.

To see Highgate Wood was once part of the great Forest of Middlesex – there are still lots of trees but there are also sports pitches, a playground and a tea shop!

To spot The disused platforms of Highgate high level station above the tube station. The tracks have all been taken up.

East Finchley

To know It was opened by the Great Northern Railway as East End, Finchley station on 22nd August 1867, and renamed East Finchley in 1887. Underground trains first used it on 3rd July 1939.

To spot Look on the roof of the station – there's a statue of an archer!

To see Cherry Tree Park, over the road from the station. From here you can watch the tube trains disappearing into the tunnel towards Highgate.

Finchley Central

To know Although the station was opened on 22nd August 1867 by the Great Northern Railway, it wasn't used by underground trains until 14th April 1940.

To spot A cattle trough – now used for growing plants – on a little island in the road opposite the entrance to the station car park.

Mill Hill East

To know The station was first used by underground trains on 18th May 1941, mainly for soldiers at the nearby barracks. The station itself was opened on 22nd August 1867 by the Great Northern Railway.

To spot The army barracks of the Royal Engineers, opposite the station.

West Finchley

To know The station was opened on 1st March 1933 by the London and North Eastern Railway and first used by underground trains on 14th April 1940.

To spot A quaint little iron footbridge over the railway track. This was moved here from a much older station which had been closed down.

Woodside Park

To know The station was first used by underground trains on 14th April 1940, but had been used for trains on the Great Northern Railway since 1872. It was originally called Torrington Park, Woodside, but was renamed Woodside Park on 1st May 1882.

To spot Can you see the cream and green station huts – do you know what they're used for?

Totteridge and Whetstone

To know The station was first used by underground trains on 14th April 1940. It was opened for main-line trains of the Great Northern Railway on 1st April 1872.

To see Apparently there's a large stone nearby where the soldiers sharpened their weapons before the Battle of Barnet in 1471. Whether you find it or not, there are some lovely walks in the fields around. Why not follow the footpath to Barnet – it takes you through some very pretty countryside.

To spot A little stream running through the parkland outside the station.

High Barnet

To know The station was first opened by the Great Northern Railway on 1st April 1872, but wasn't used by underground trains until 14th April 1940.

To see The Battle of Barnet was fought here in 1471 – the Earl of Warwick was killed and his army beaten. There's an obelisk to mark the spot on Hadley Common, a 15 minute walk from the station. You'll find out more about the battle in the Barnet Museum (Wood Street, Barnet Tel: 01-449 0321 x4). There are all sorts of other interesting things in this little museum including a collection of horseshoes from the middle ages onwards and an exhibition of Brazilian butterflies.

To spot The weather vane on top of the Court House will tell you which way the wind is blowing. Walk up the steep lane and look to your right.

PICCADILLY LINE

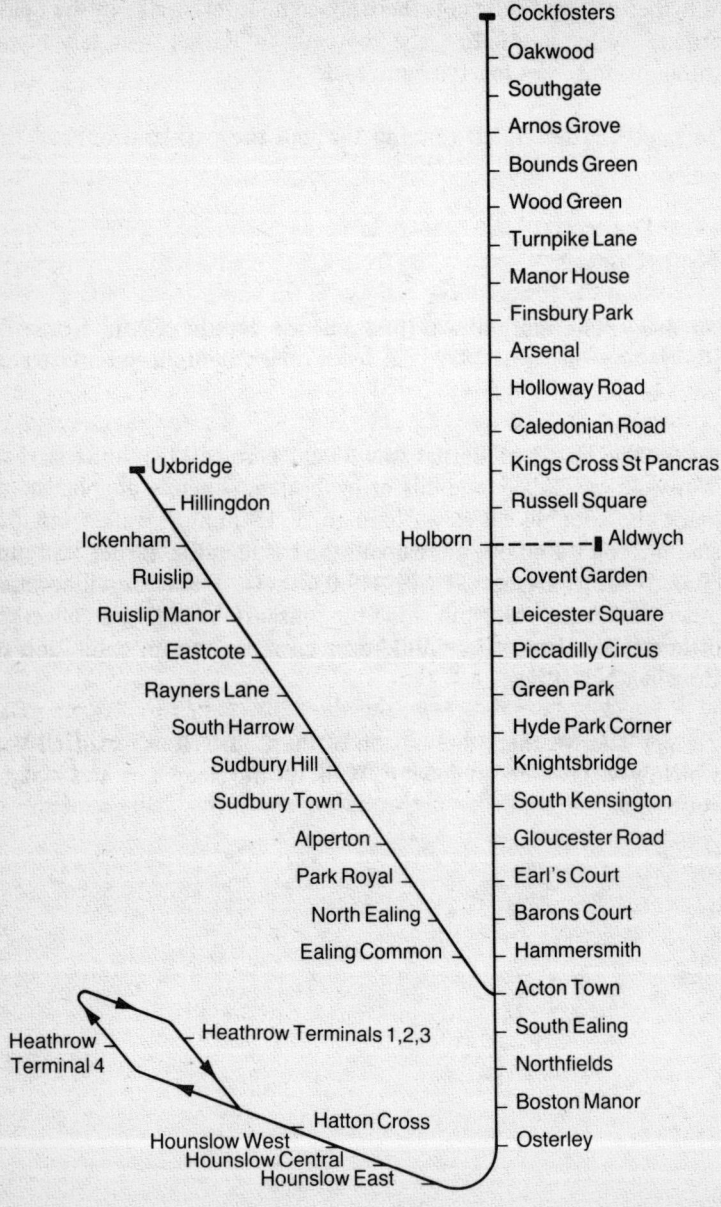

- Cockfosters
- Oakwood
- Southgate
- Arnos Grove
- Bounds Green
- Wood Green
- Turnpike Lane
- Manor House
- Finsbury Park
- Arsenal
- Holloway Road
- Caledonian Road
- Kings Cross St Pancras
- Russell Square

Uxbridge
Hillingdon
Ickenham
Ruislip
Ruislip Manor
Eastcote
Rayners Lane
South Harrow
Sudbury Hill
Sudbury Town
Alperton
Park Royal
North Ealing
Ealing Common

Holborn — — — — Aldwych
- Covent Garden
- Leicester Square
- Piccadilly Circus
- Green Park
- Hyde Park Corner
- Knightsbridge
- South Kensington
- Gloucester Road
- Earl's Court
- Barons Court
- Hammersmith
- Acton Town
- South Ealing
- Northfields
- Boston Manor
- Osterley

Heathrow
Terminal 4
Heathrow Terminals 1,2,3
Hatton Cross
Hounslow West
Hounslow Central
Hounslow East

The **Piccadilly Line** was opened in December 1906 by Lloyd George. The first section was from Finsbury Park to Hammersmith, making it the longest tube railway at the time. It was also different in that it had fares ranging from 1d to 4d instead of a flat fare of 2d. A branch was opened in 1907 from Holborn to Strand (Aldwych). In the 1930s it was extended north to Cockfosters and west to Hounslow and Uxbridge. Then in 1977 the Queen opened the extension to Heathrow Central making Heathrow the first international airport in the world to be directly linked with a city centre by underground railway.

On 14th April 1986, there were new events on the Piccadilly Line. Heathrow Central changed its name to Heathrow Terminals 1, 2, 3, and a four mile loop was opened linking a new station, Heathrow Terminal 4, with Hatton Cross. This was opened by the Prince and Princess of Wales.

With the new extensions, the Piccadilly Line now covers nearly 40 route miles and serves 51 stations. It runs from the Heathrow Terminal stations to Cockfosters in the north and to Uxbridge in the west. A peak hour shuttle service runs from Holborn to Aldwych.

Heathrow Terminal 4

To know This is the newest station on the underground and it serves the new terminal at Heathrow. It was opened on 14th April 1986 by the Prince and Princess of Wales. It's on a four mile loop from Hatton Cross (see below).

Heathrow Terminals 1, 2 and 3

To know The station was opened on 16th December 1977. It was renamed Heathrow Terminals 1, 2, 3, when the new underground station was opened at Heathrow Terminal 4.

To see Calling all plane-spotters! Heathrow is the busiest international airport in the world and from the Spectators' Roof Gardens on top of the Queen's Building, you can see all the planes from all parts of the world landing, departing and taxiing. There's always something to see but keep a special look-out for Concorde!

To spot A yellow, blue and white aeroplane – well a picture of one! You can see the tail-end on the underground platform.

Hatton Cross

To know The station was opened on 19th July 1975.

To spot Stand in the car park for some spectacular views of aeroplanes arriving and leaving Heathrow Airport.

Hounslow West

To know The station was opened as Hounslow Barracks on 21st July 1884. It was renamed Hounslow West on 1st December 1925 and a new station was opened on 11th December 1926.

Hounslow Central

To know When the station was opened on 1st April 1886 it was known as Heston Hounslow. A second station was opened on 19th October 1912, and the name was changed to Hounslow Central on 1st December 1925.

Hounslow East

To know The very first station to open near here was on a spur line on 1st May 1883. It was called Hounslow then renamed Hounslow Town in 1884. It was closed in March 1886 but reopened in March 1903. It was finally closed on 1st May 1909 and the next day, a new station on the main Piccadilly Line was opened. It was given the name Hounslow East on 1st December 1925.

To spot There's a tiny little waiting room on the westbound platform. How many people do you think would fit inside it?

Osterley

To know The original station near here was called Osterley and Spring Grove, and opened on 1st May 1883. However, it was resited and a new station opened on 25th March 1934 as Osterley. Can you see the earlier station? It's still there. You will pass it if you walk to Osterley Park. What is the old station building used for now?

To see You're very near to Osterley Park – once described as 'well wooded, and garnished with manie faire ponds'. It's lovely! In the park is Osterley Park House (Tel: 01-560 3918), a beautiful old mansion.

To spot A tree in the island by the bus stop outside the station. Can you find out what kind of tree it is?

Boston Manor

To know This station was first Boston Road when it was opened in May 1883, but was given the grander title Boston Manor on 11th December 1911. It was rebuilt and re-opened on 25th March 1934.

To spot The Great Pagoda at Kew Gardens (see page 65). Stand on the westernmost end of the westbound platform and look very carefully.

Northfields

To know The original station was opened as Northfield (Ealing) on 16th April 1908. However, it was resited and called Northfields on 19th May 1932.

To spot Some little wooden seats in the alcoves on the platform – very comfy for waiting for your train.

South Ealing

To know The station was opened on 1st May 1883.

To spot An old wooden clock on the eastbound platform.

Acton Town (see District Line page 64)

Hammersmith (see District Line page 68)

Baron's Court (see District Line page 68)

Earl's Court (see District Line page 60)

Gloucester Road (see Circle Line page 44)

South Kensington (see Circle Line page 45)

Knightsbridge

To know The station was opened on 15th December 1906. There's a story that centuries ago knights used to have their jousting tournaments on the area around a nearby bridge – hence the name!

To see Welcome to Harrods! It's London's most famous department store. Make sure you visit the Food Halls in the middle of the store which have beautiful tiled walls and an amazing display of fresh fish.

Hyde Park Corner

To know The station was opened on 15th December 1906.

To see This is the start of the annual London to Brighton Veteran Car Run, so if you're here on the first Sunday in November watch these beautifully maintained old cars take to the road. This is a once-a-year event, but The Wellington Museum (Apsley House, 149 Piccadilly W1 Tel: 01-499 5676) is open all the year round. It was the Duke of Wellington's home and has lots of his personal relics, including a handwritten despatch from the Battle of Waterloo. When he lived here it was known as 'No 1, London'.

To spot The 1st Duke of Wellington himself – well, a statue anyway! He's riding his famous horse called 'Copenhagen'.

Green Park (see Jubilee Line page 78)

Piccadilly Circus (see Bakerloo Line page 14)

Leicester Square (see Northern Line page 107)

Covent Garden

To know This station is said to be haunted! The figure of actor William Terris is said to wander its platforms. Terris was stabbed to death, in 1897, at the Adelphi Theatre by a jealous fellow actor – but no one knows why he waits for the underground train! The station was opened here on 11th April 1907.

To see Try out the controls of a bus and a train, or work the signals in the London Transport Museum (Covent Garden WC2 Tel: 01-379 6344). Next door is the Theatre Museum (Tel: 01-586 6371 x 372) with all kinds of exhibits from the world of the stage.

Covent Garden, once a fruit and vegetable market, is now a popular and lively pedestrian piazza full of cafés, boutiques and colourful craft stalls. Around lunch time you can watch buskers put on a show in front of St Paul's Church – they're very professional. In fact they have to audition to be allowed to perform.

To spot The place where the first Punch and Judy show was held is marked by a special plaque.

Holborn (see Central Line page 32)

Aldwych

To know During the years of World War II, the tunnel between Aldwych and Holborn (see page 32) stations was used not by tube trains, but as a storehouse for treasures from the British Museum!

Opened as Strand on 30th November 1907, the station was renamed Aldwych on 9th May 1915.

To see Walk down Surrey Street and you'll reach the Victoria Embankment (WC2) beside the river Thames. Walking along towards Westminster Bridge and Big Ben, you'll pass Cleopatra's Needle. This huge obelisk some 68½ feet (20.8 metres) high is made from granite. Dating back to 1500 BC, it was brought to London from Egypt in 1877 and is the oldest monument in London.

To spot The entrance to King's College is just beside the tube station.

Russell Square

To know The station was opened on 15th December 1906.

To see London has many, many, squares – areas of greenery flanked by terraces of houses. Two of its more interesting squares – Russell Square and Tavistock Square – are near the underground station. Russell Square has some unusual fountains and Tavistock Square is known for its statue of Mahatma Gandhi (1869–1948).

To spot The Brunswick Shopping Centre. It is an unusual construction and students of architecture often come here to study it. So if you think you may one day want to be an architect, take a look at this building!

Kings Cross St Pancras (see Circle Line page 55)

Caledonian Road

To know In 1826 there was an asylum for Scottish children here. It was called the Caledonian Asylum which is how the station, which was opened on 15th December 1906, got its name.

To spot A picture of a little church in the tile work of the station – just outside the lift.

Holloway Road

To know The station was opened on 15th December 1906.

Arsenal

To know Arsenal Football Club is the only club to have an underground station named after it. The station was opened as Gillespie Road on 15th December 1906 but was renamed Arsenal on 31st October 1932 when the club had become so successful.

To see Whether you're an Arsenal supporter or not, a tour of Arsenal Football Stadium is really fascinating. You can see the changing rooms, treatment rooms, the Board Room and press room and get a really close look at the pitch. And there's all the trophies and medals too. To book a tour you should write to: Tour Manager, Arsenal Stadium, Avenell Road, London N5.

Finsbury Park

To know The main-line station was opened by the Great Northern Railway on 1st July 1861 as Seven Sisters Road, Holloway. It was renamed Finsbury Park in 1869. The first underground station was opened on 14th February 1904 by the Great Northern and City Railway. The Piccadilly Line platforms were opened on 15th December 1906 and the Victoria Line on 1st September 1968.

To see Finsbury Park is one of London's oldest parks, and one of the busiest too! There's a playground and playpark, a boating lake and lots of sports going on. The Michael Sobell Sports Centre (Hornsey Road, N7 Tel: 01-607 1632) is nearby too. There are special sessions for young people.

To spot On the southbound Victoria Line platform, there's a picture in the tiles of two guns crossed over a tree. This represents the duels that used to be fought in the park. What can you see on the northbound platform? Look out for the mosaic balloons on the Piccadilly Line platforms. Hot air balloons once took off from Finsbury Park.

Manor House

To know The station was opened on 19th September 1932.

To see You'll find an animal enclosure with an aviary full of colourful tropical birds in Clissold Park, just a short walk down Green Lanes.

To spot Manor House itself! It's right beside the station.

Turnpike Lane

To know The station was opened on 19th September 1932. A 'turnpike' gate where tolls were paid by road users, used to stand nearby.

To spot The decorated ventilation grilles along the station platforms. What do they show?

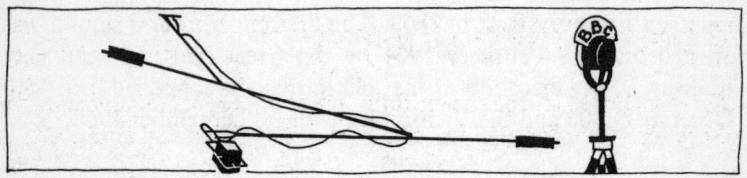

Wood Green

To know The station was opened on 19th September 1932.

To see Alexandra Park is a great place to spend an afternoon – there's a boating lake, a pitch and putt course, an animal enclosure and a super adventure playground. Have fun! It was from Alexandra Palace that the world's first regular television broadcast was made by the BBC on 2nd November 1936.

Bounds Green

To know The station was opened on 19th September 1932.

To spot Two tall, strange-shaped lamps at the bottom of the escalator.

Arnos Grove

To know The station was opened on 19th September 1932.

To see Broomfield Park with a model boat pond and three lakes where you can feed the ducks is nearby. Broomfield House, an ancient mansion in the park, is now a museum (Tel: 01-882 1354) with an amazing collection of stuffed animals and birds. Upstairs there's a Victorian nursery full of toys and games the children used to play with.

Southgate

To know It was opened on 13th March 1933.

To spot Look at the beautifully polished bronze lamps on the escalator – it makes you feel like royalty as you ride up and down.

Oakwood

To know When the station opened on 13th March 1933 it was called Enfield West. It became known as Oakwood on 1st September 1946.

Cockfosters

To know The station was opened on 31st July 1933.

To see The wonderful Trent Park is very near. It covers over 400 acres of parks and woods with a nature trail so you can discover all the wildlife. Don't miss Fernyhill Farm – you can find out what happens on a real working farm.

To spot At the station entrance, a message in braille for blind people. It's the start of a special Woodland Trail so blind people can enjoy the park.

Ealing Common (see District Line page 63)

North Ealing

To know The station was opened on 23rd June 1903.

Park Royal

To know The station was opened as Park Royal and Twyford Abbey on 23rd June 1903. It was resited and changed its name to Park Royal on 6th July 1931. A new station was built by the same architects as the shops, hotel and houses nearby, and opened in 1936.

To spot Before World War I there was a plan to try and make a large piece of land (where the station now stands) into a ground for the Royal Agricultural Society Annual Show. The project failed and the land was built on – but you *can* see cows and horses belonging to the Guinness Brewery put out to graze on a patch of grass opposite the station! The Brewery is the huge brick building a bit farther away.

Alperton

To know The station was opened as Perivale-Alperton on 28th June 1903 then as Alperton on 7th October 1910.

Sudbury Town

To know The station was opened on 28th June 1903. It was the first of the Piccadilly Line stations to be rebuilt, in 1931. All the other stations built or rebuilt in the 1930s look very similar. The architect, Charles Holden, called the style 'a brick box with a concrete lid'!

To see Feel like playing some sport? Well, the Vale Farm Sports Centre isn't far away in Watford Road, Wembley (Tel: 01-908 2528). It's the home of the Middlesex Ladies Athletics Club so you might see some really good athletics on the running track.

To spot A weather-vane high on the wall inside the booking hall – it looks like a clock!

Sudbury Hill

To know The station was opened on 28th June 1903.

To spot A huge London Transport sign in the glass panelling above the station entrance.

South Harrow

To know The station was opened on 28th June 1903. It was resited on 5th July 1935.

To spot There's a huge grey building nearby. Do you know what it is used for?

Rayners Lane (see Metropolitan Line page 93)

Eastcote (see Metropolitan Line page 93)

Ruislip Manor (see Metropolitan Line page 93)

Ruislip (see Metropolitan Line page 93)

Ickenham (see Metropolitan Line page 93)

Hillingdon (see Metropolitan Line page 94)

Uxbridge (see Metropolitan Line page 94)

VICTORIA LINE

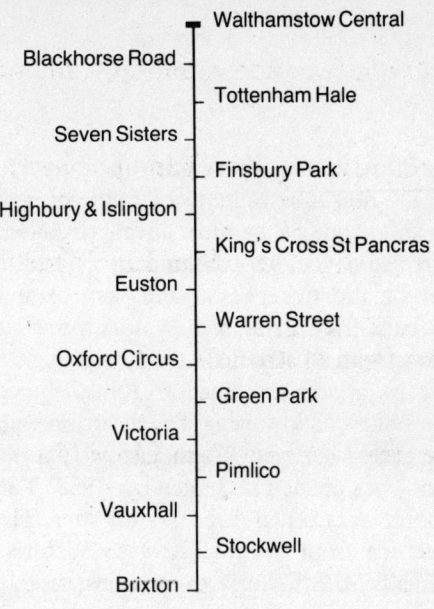

Walthamstow Central
Blackhorse Road
Tottenham Hale
Seven Sisters
Finsbury Park
Highbury & Islington
King's Cross St Pancras
Euston
Warren Street
Oxford Circus
Green Park
Victoria
Pimlico
Vauxhall
Stockwell
Brixton

The **Victoria Line** is the newest tube line, apart from the Jubilee Line. It was the first tube route to be built across Central London since 1907 – and is one of the most advanced railways in the whole world. Right from the very beginning it had automatic train operation, automatic ticket issue and control and closed circuit television. It runs from Brixton to Walthamstow Central and is 14 route miles long with 16 stations.

Work first began on the line on 20th September 1962. The tunnels were built quickly using a new 'drum digging' technique and the first part – between Walthamstow Central and Highbury and Islington – was opened in September 1968. The second section to Warren Street was opened three months later. The Queen opened the Victoria Line from Walthamstow to Victoria on 7th March 1969. And finally, the Victoria to Brixton section was opened on 23rd July 1971 by Princess Alexandra, giving us the Victoria Line we know today.

Brixton

To know The underground station was opened here on 23rd July 1971.

To see You can visit a windmill in Brixton! (Blenheim Gardens, SW2 Tel: 01-671 2907.) It was built in 1816 and you can still see pieces of machinery which were used then including: the bedstone, a wallower and the spur wheel. A big diagram on the wall will tell you what those things are and what they do.

There's also a colourful market in Brixton, very near to the underground station (Electric Avenue, SW9). It's particularly busy on Saturday mornings when you'll be able to see all sorts of fruits and vegetables being sold. You may not be able to recognise some of them!

Stockwell (see Northern Line page 104)

Vauxhall

To know The station was opened on 23rd July 1971.

To see New Covent Garden Market (Nine Elms Lane, SW8) is a huge wholesale market selling fruit and vegetables. But *you* can't buy anything here; this is where greengrocers buy their produce by the box load, not the pound! Trading starts early – it's a very busy place by 6.00 A.M. so that the greengrocers can have their wares on display when the shops open at 9.00 A.M. It's an exciting place to visit but you'll probably have to persuade an adult to go with you.

To spot On nearby Vauxhall Bridge you can see what the Thames watermen have called 'Little St Paul's on the Water' – a miniature of St Paul's Cathedral.

Pimlico

To know The station was opened on 14th September 1972.

To see The Tate Gallery (Millbank, SW1 Tel: 01-821 1313) is one of Britain's major art galleries. There are hundreds of sculptures and paintings here dating from the 16th century to the present day. Try drawing your favourite picture. Or, when you get home, make your own piece of modern sculpture.

To spot Walking from the underground station to the Tate Gallery you'll pass a sculpture of a ballet dancer. Which sculptor made it?

Victoria (see Circle Line page 47)

Green Park (see Jubilee Line page 78)

Oxford Circus (see Bakerloo Line page 15)

Warren Street (see Northern Line page 108)

Euston (see Northern Line page 109)

Kings Cross St Pancras (see Circle Line page 55)

Highbury and Islington

To know An overground station called Islington was opened here by the North London Railway on 26th September 1850. The first underground station was opened here by the Great Northern and City Railway on 28th June 1904 and called Highbury. It was renamed Highbury and Islington on 20th July 1922. The Victoria Line platforms were opened on 1st September 1968.

To spot The clock and tower of the Union Chapel (Upper Street, N1). If you look inside you can spot something else – a piece of Pilgrim Rock from the place where the settlers in North America first landed.

Finsbury Park (see Piccadilly Line page 127)

Seven Sisters

To know It was opened on 1st September 1968.

To see You must go to Bruce Castle Museum (Lordship Lane, Tottenham N17 Tel: 01-808 8772)! It's got a wonderful collection of everything to do with stamps and postal history including an early postboy's riding boots and hat, some rare letter boxes and special documents. There's also a Military Museum with the uniforms, weapons and equipment which used to belong to the Middlesex Regiment.

To spot On the Victoria Line northbound platform there are some tiles with little trees against a green background. Why trees at Seven Sisters? Well, the road took its name, not from seven sisters but from seven elm trees which grew nearby!

Tottenham Hale

To know The station was opened on 1st September 1968.

To spot Yourself! There's a huge mirror in the booking hall.

Blackhorse Road

To know The station was opened on 1st September 1968.

To spot A black horse, of course! There's one carved in the wall just outside the station entrance. Look for the ribbon in its tail.

Walthamstow Central

To know Underground trains began running to this station on 1st September 1968, however there has been a main-line station here since 1870.

To see William Morris, a famous designer and craftsman was born in Walthamstow in 1834. His family home is now a museum called the William Morris Gallery (Lloyd Park, Forest Road, E17 Tel: 01-527 5544 x 4390) and has examples of his designs for furniture, fabrics, wallpaper and church decorations. Look out for the wood blocks used for handprinting cloth.

To spot As a tribute to William Morris there's one of his designs in the tiles on the platform wall.

DO YOU KNOW?

You'll find the answers to all the questions below somewhere in the book.

Which underground station has the deepest lift shaft?

Which station has the shortest escalator?

The longest tube journey you can make without changing trains is 31.4 miles (54.9 km). Between which stations does it stretch?

At which station do you get off to visit the London Transport Museum?

From which bridge over the Thames can you spot the 'Oxo' Tower?

The longest continuous tunnel, some 17 miles 528 yards (27.842 km), is between which two stations?

Which south London underground station recieved a direct hit during bombing in World War II?

The shortest distance between two stations is 0.16 miles (0.26 km). What are the names of the stations?

Beside which two tube stations can you spot cattle troughs?

At which station do you get off the tube to see the home of the Lord Mayor of London?

Which station has the most escalators? How many are there?

Which is the only football club to have a station named after it?

Who opened the Jubilee Line in 1979?

If you wanted to visit the Natural History Museum which station would you get off at?

There's a stone which marks the place where Dick Whittington heard the Bow Bells telling him to go back to London. Which station is it near?

Who helped to encourage people to travel on the first escalator at an underground station?

Which four letters of the alphabet don't have a tube station beginning with them?

Which tube line was known as the 'Tuppenny Tube' when it was first opened?

Which station has a river flowing over it?

Which station has the biggest car park? How many car spaces are there?

Fiction in paperback from Dragon Books

Mr T	£1.50	☐
Ann Jungman		
Vlad the Drac	£1.25	☐
Vlad the Drac Returns	£1.25	☐
Vlad the Drac Superstar	£1.50	☐
Jane Holiday		
Gruesome and Bloodsocks	£1.25	☐
Thomas Meehan		
Annie	£1.50	☐
Michael Denton		
Eggbox Brontosaurus	£1.25	☐
Glitter City	£1.25	☐
Fantastic	£1.25	☐
Marika Hanbury Tenison		
The Princess and the Unicorn	£1.25	☐
Alan Davidson		
A Friend Like Annabel	£1.25	☐
Just Like Annabel	£1.25	☐
Maureen Spurgeon		
BMX Bikers	£1.50	☐
BMX Bikers and the Dirt-Track Racers	£1.50	☐
T R Burch		
Ben and Blackbeard	£1.25	☐
Ben on Cole's Hill	£1.25	☐
Jonathan Rumbold		
The Adventures of Niko	£1.25	☐
Marcus Crouch		
The Ivory City	95p	☐
Lynne Reid Banks		
The Indian in the Cupboard	£1.50	☐
Nina Beachcroft		
A Spell of Sleep	£1.25	☐
Cold Christmas	£1.50	☐
Graham Marks		
The Finding of Stoby Binder	£1.50	☐
David Osborn		
Jessica and the Crocodile Knight	£1.50	☐

To order direct from the publisher just tick the titles you want
and fill in the order form.

Fiction in paperback from Dragon Books

Peter Glidewell

Schoolgirl Chums	£1.25	☐
St Ursula's in Danger	£1.25	☐
Miss Prosser's Passion	£1.50	☐

Enid Gibson

The Lady at 99	£1.50	☐

Gerald Frow

Young Sherlock: The Mystery of the Manor House	95p	☐
Young Sherlock: The Adventure at Ferryman's Creek	£1.50	☐

Frank Richards

Billy Bunter of Greyfriars School	£1.25	☐
Billy Bunter's Double	£1.25	☐
Billy Bunter Comes for Christmas	£1.25	☐
Billy Bunter Does His Best	£1.25	☐
Billy Bunter's Benefit	£1.50	☐
Billy Bunter's Postal Order	£1.50	☐

Dale Carlson
Jenny Dean Mysteries

Mystery of the Shining Children	£1.50	☐
Mystery of the Hidden Trap	£1.50	☐
Secret of the Third Eye	£1.50	☐

Marlene Fanta Shyer

My Brother the Thief	95p	☐

David Rees

The Exeter Blitz	£1.50	☐

Caroline Akrill

Eventer's Dream	£1.50	☐
A Hoof in the Door	£1.50	☐
Ticket to Ride	£1.50	☐

Michel Parry (ed)

Superheroes	£1.25	☐

Ulick O'Connor

Irish Tales and Sagas	£2.95	☐

To order direct from the publisher just tick the titles you want
and fill in the order form.

All these books are available at your local bookshop or newsagent, or can be ordered direct from the publisher.

To order direct from the publishers just tick the titles you want and fill in the form below.

Name _____

Address _____

_____

Send to:
Dragon Cash Sales
PO Box 11, Falmouth, Cornwall TR10 9EN.

Please enclose remittance to the value of the cover price plus:

UK 45p for the first book, 20p for the second book plus 14p per copy for each additional book ordered to a maximum charge of £1.63.

BFPO and Eire 45p for the first book, 20p for the second book plus 14p per copy for the next 7 books, thereafter 8p per book.

Overseas 75p for the first book and 21p for each additional book.

Dragon Books reserve the right to show new retail prices on covers, which may differ from those previously advertised in the text or elsewhere.